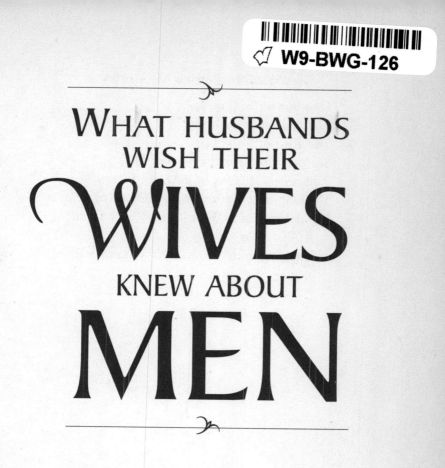

WHAT HUSBANDS WISH THEIR

WIVES

KNEW ABOUT

MEN

Resources by Patrick M. Morley

Devotions for Couples
The Man in the Mirror
The Rest of Your Life
Second Wind for the Second Half
The Seven Seasons of a Man's Life
Walking with Christ in the Details of Life
What Husbands Wish Their Wives Knew
  About Men
What Husbands Wish Their Wives Knew
  About Men audio

WHAT HUSBANDS WISH THEIR

WIVES

KNEW ABOUT

MEN

Author of the best-selling
THE MAN IN THE MIRROR

PATRICK M. MORLEY

ZondervanPublishingHouse
Grand Rapids, Michigan

A Division of HarperCollinsPublishers

What Husbands Wish Their Wives Knew About Men
Copyright © 1998 by Patrick M. Morley

Requests for information should be addressed to:

📖 ZondervanPublishingHouse
Grand Rapids, Michigan 49530

Library of Congress Cataloging-in-Publication Data

Morley, Patrick M.
    What husbands wish their wives knew about men / Patrick M. Morley.
        p.   cm.
    ISBN: 0-310-22909-X (softcover)
    1. Husbands—Psychology. 2. Marriage. 3. Man-woman relationships.
    I. Title.
    HQ756.M67   1997
    360.872—dc21   97-37316
                                                  CIP

Published in association with the literary agency of Wolgemuth and Associates, Inc.

Interior design by Sherri L. Hoffman

Printed in the United States of America

01 02 03 /❖ DC/ 10 9 8 7 6

Marriage is a learned thing.

Some learn it well.

Others don't.

Thanks to my parents,

Bob and Alleen Morley,

and my wife's parents,

Ed and June Cole,

I learned by observation how to

truly love and respect my wife, Patsy.

Thank you.

For this and countless other reasons

I dedicate this book to you.

Contents ৵

Part Three

Introduction ✒

Sometimes, when she awakens before her husband, she will roll over and gaze curiously at the strange creature with gaping mouth who softly snores on the pillow next to hers.

Puzzling, nettlesome questions tumble through her mind: *Who is this man I married? What makes him tick? Why isn't he more responsive to my needs? Did he change, or did I just not understand him in the first place?*

Unknown to her, some days, when he awakens first, he will stare adoringly at his bride, baffled by his impotence to share more deeply with this woman he loves so much. *Why can't I find the words to tell her what's in my heart—how much I love her, my hopes and dreams for us, the things that scare me, my good intentions, and how sorry I am for the ways I've let the family down?*

But such words don't come readily. Besides, he must get up now and go track his bear. There are bills to pay, customers to serve, calls to return, deals to be done, and many miles to cover before his thoughts can return once again to such matters of the heart.

WHAT MEN ARE LIKE

I work with men as a vocation. Far and away the number-one problem men face today is that their marriages are not working the way they are supposed to. That is why I wanted to write this book.

In these pages I would like to take you aside and show you some things you ought to know about men. My goal is to tell you what a man is like from a man's perspective—what he's feeling inside, what he's thinking, and what he's going through. Men need a spokesperson to convey some things to their wives. I would like to attempt the role of "translator" for men. I want to take you inside "the locker room." So whether you are married, engaged, single, or single again, by the time you finish reading this book I believe you will know how men are "wired."

Far and away the number-one problem men face today is that their marriages are not working the way they are supposed to.

My greatest wish would be that a man could read this book and say, "Yes! He's articulating exactly what I'm feeling. Honey, would you read this book so you'll understand me better?"

PERSPECTIVE

Since four thoughts kept ringing in my ears and became the controlling ideas for this book, I thought you should know up front where I'm coming from:

1. *Marriage is a good thing*. Marriage blesses. Marriage is that mysterious, spiritual fusion of two separate lives headed in two separate directions into one flesh.

2. *All relationships are difficult, especially marriage*. I once heard Florence Littauer say, "We are attracted to marry each other's strengths, and then go home to live with each other's weaknesses." Two people rubbing against each other every day are bound to create some friction. Love is the glue that can hold us together and the oil that can keep us from rubbing each other the wrong way.

3. *Virtually all men believe that they are, or have been, a difficult husband to live with.* Most likely, many regrets haunt your husband. He knows he has been a difficult man to be around. Yet he wants to make up the years he robbed from you.

4. *Most men have it in their hearts to do the right thing.* Based on hundreds of surveys and thousands of interviews I would say the overwhelming conclusion is this: Most men really want to do the right

Most men have it in their hearts to do the right thing.

thing. Men deeply love their wives. Along the way they have bought into a few ideas that knocked them off balance, but their hearts are good.

To prepare for writing this volume I conducted two years of extensive research among men and women alike, including written surveys and personal interviews. I also taught a series of the same title to 150 men in Orlando over a four-month period.

The stories you will read are real, though some details and names have been disguised where appropriate.

In any chapter you may experience "role reversal." In other words, what's said about your husband may sound more like you, and vice versa. Since addressing such differences is beyond the scope of this book, let me encourage you to make any needed adjustments in your own mind.

A special word of thanks to Jim Dobson for giving me his blessing to use the title for this book, since it closely resembles and is the inverse of his best-selling 1973 book, *What Wives Wish Their Husbands Knew About Women.*

To make this book as practical as possible I've added a section, "How You Can Help Your Husband," at the end of each chapter. Also, there's a section, "A Thought for Husbands," that you can show to your husband and ask him to mull over.

One final word. R. C. Sproul concluded the foreword to *The Man in the Mirror* in good humor by saying to men, "If someone gives you this book or if you buy it yourself, be sure to read it. If you don't read it, by all means destroy it before your wife gets hold of it. If the unthinkable happens, if you don't read it, and your wife does, then my dear brother, you are in deep weeds." This then, wives, is *The Man in the Mirror: Women's Edition.*

Part One

One ༄

Childhood

"What I Know I Learned from My Dad"

It was a touching scene as Michael Jordan fell to the floor, buried his face in his hands, and sobbed on national television. The Chicago Bulls had just earned their fourth NBA basketball championship in six years.

Why was Michael Jordan, arguably the greatest athlete of our generation, weeping? Were they tears of joy for the ultimate achievement? Was it a release from the pressure of all the media hype?

No, it was Father's Day.

To understand this odyssey to the pinnacle of sports success we must dissolve back to three years earlier when Michael Jordan's father, James, was brutally murdered in a story that captured headlines everywhere.

Not long after his father's untimely death, Michael abruptly retired from basketball. Michael Jordan's sudden departure from hoops at the height of his career, his brief encounter with baseball, and his eventual triumphant return to the parquet floors of basketball have been attributed to many causes.

Yet, only one opinion makes sense. This young man had lost his daddy. Michael Jordan loved his father. His dad was his hero, a mentor, and a friend. In his grief Michael stumbled over the inevitable lurking questions about life's larger meaning and purpose. Like any of us might do, he lost his bearings for a season.

But life goes on, and God is kind. Time heals. Perspective returns. Things get back to where they were. And Michael Jordan came back to basketball.

As Jordan made possibly the greatest sports comeback in history, he dedicated his comeback season to his father, James. After a storybook year, Jordan and the Chicago Bulls found themselves standing on the brink of winning the NBA championship title on Father's Day.

Just before game time Jordan reflected on the possibility of winning the championship on Father's Day: "It would be very gratifying, a tribute to my father and the motivation he has provided. Even though he hasn't been around, that's part of my motivation every day, to go out and make him proud."[1]

So there he lay, perhaps the greatest sports hero of our time, heaving long sobs as he thought of his father.

What motivates a man? Complex question. Perhaps no man can reach into his own heart and pull out the exact words to describe what gets him out of bed in the morning.

One motive, however, compels men like few others. It is foundational, perpetual, and insatiable. I speak of your husband's need for his dad to be proud of him.

HOW FATHERS INFLUENCE THEIR SONS

J remember my son, John, as a miniature five-year-old tike, wrapping his towel around himself after a shower just like I do, then mimicking my rituals of shaving, brushing my teeth, and combing my wet hair.

A little boy has a special bond with his dad. This is how God planned it. God wants fathers to use this "genetic" influence to mold and shape their sons and daughters. The Bible tells us ...

> These commandments that I give you today are to be upon your hearts. Impress them on your children. Talk about them when you sit at home and when you walk along the road, when you lie down and when you get up. Tie them as symbols on your hands and bind them on your foreheads. Write them on the doorframes of your houses and on your gates (Deuteronomy 6:6–9).

In today's culture we might say, "Talk after you finish watching TV together about the show's message; discuss Sunday's sermon when you are driving in your car; read Bible stories at bedtime; and have family devotions in the morning before everyone heads off in different directions for the day. Keep reminders of the Lord, such as Christian music, books, and art, around your home. Develop and maintain friendships with other Christians."

A little boy has a special bond with his dad. This is how God planned it.

Did your husband's father build into his life like this?

Nothing has influenced your husband more than his relationship with his own earthly father. The seemingly small ripples of your father-in-law's influence pound perpetually like ocean waves against the pilings of your husband's view of the world, himself, and you.

Engaged women, do you want to know how your fiancé will treat you in marriage? Observe how his father treats his mother. If well, it will be a blessing to you. If badly, does your fiancé know something is wrong? Is he prepared to break with the past? Ask him, "What have you learned by watching the way your father treats and mistreats your mother?"

HOW FATHERS INFLUENCE THEIR SONS

Your father-in-law influenced your husband in one of four different ways:

Your father-in-law may have had no influence on your husband. Perhaps your husband's father was absent because of death, divorce, or abandonment. My own dad's father, for example, abandoned his family when my dad was only four years old.

While some of the world's best husbands emerge from these circumstances, it's far more likely to make life a struggle. Fatherless men suffer because they lack the warmth and affection of a father's love and the empathy for others inbred by a healthy childhood experience. Instead, they must look exclusively to their mothers. Hopefully, God also brought another father figure into their lives.

Men need fathers, and they suffer when they don't have one. One day a young inner-city boy seemed unusually sad to a youth center worker. "What's wrong?" the youth worker asked.

"Nuthin'," he said.

"Come on, you look so sad. You can tell me."

"Well-ll,... okay." He hesitated, then added, "It's my dad."

"What about your dad?" the youth worker asked.

"I don't have one. Can't do nuthin' without a dad," said the little boy.

Your father-in-law may have had a neutral or small influence on your husband. Bill grew up in the cold north country, the ninth child of his father. His people were a rugged lot. They struggled to make ends meet. Bill said, "My father didn't really have that much of an influence on me. Oh, he was a decent man—a good man, actually. But he was just not into fathering. He was always preoccupied, distant. I never really knew much about him."

Many men feel their fathers were "distant" when they grew up, even if they're "tight" with their fathers today. Not a few men grew up in homes where dad thought he was doing the right thing by devoting himself to the American Dream at the expense of time with his kids. These fathers were not bad men, they simply weren't around. Maybe it was work, or a hobby or a sport. Maybe he was a couch potato. He wasn't a bad guy, but his influence was "small." Today, regrets stalk most of those men who didn't carve out more time for fathering. Today, perhaps because of our father's mistakes, our culture has become much more father/son friendly.

Nevertheless, these men often influenced their sons—perhaps your husband—to throw themselves into their work or some other activity that takes them out of the daily flow of family life. He's just not with it. Following in their father's footsteps, many men today are hopelessly preoccupied with work, sports, and hobbies.

Your father-in-law may have been a negative role model for your husband. While I believe most men have it in their hearts to do the right thing, husbands often repeat the sins of their fathers: "Like father, like son." Sometimes men grew up around fathers entangled in destructive behaviors such as alcohol, verbal, and even physical abuse. These men took the brunt of their father's anger. Maybe they watched helplessly as their parents divorced, often feeling at fault.

Some men, like a friend of mine, heard shattering words. His dad repeatedly said to him, "You're stupid.... You're no good.... You'll never amount to anything." Then, that fragile little boy spends the rest of his life trying to prove that his father was either right or wrong. It is a powerful, though often crippling, motivator.

Your father-in-law may have been a positive role model for your husband. Last year the father of a good friend slumped over with a heart attack while planting new seedling pines on his farm. A few minutes later the hospital pronounced him DOA at the age of fifty-seven. Though his life was taken early, he passed his blessing along to his son. I asked my friend, "What do you remember most about your dad?"

Without missing a beat he said, "My dad did not leave any unfinished business. He was forceful about making sure he told me, 'I love you' and 'I'm proud of you.' I heard it all the time.

"My dad accepted me unconditionally. When I tried out for football my dad said, 'If you want to play, fine. If not, that's fine, too.' My dad spent a lot of time on the road, but he was there for every single athletic event. Even if he had to drive two hours to be there, even if he was late, he was there. Now I realize how much I took that for granted. Many of the dads of the other kids never came to a game, not one."

Wives, your husband was sculpted, for better or worse, by the father he had, or the one who wasn't around. He was crafted by the example of that man who gave him life.

A QUIZ FOR WIVES

Let's take a quiz to see how well you can describe your husband's father. Put a "check" next to the following words that strongly describe your husband's father (you can check as many as you want).

___ permissive	___ strict
___ angry	___ selfish
___ strong	___ mean
___ unknown	___ absent
___ involved	___ preoccupied
___ good	___ spiritual

___ mentor   ___ friend
___ hardworking   ___ supportive

Now, go back through the same list and put an "x" next to the descriptions which capture the kind of father your husband has become. See what I mean?

Let's continue the quiz. Put a "check" next to the following characteristics that strongly describe the way your husband's father treated his wife (again, you can check as many as you want).

___ affectionate   ___ preoccupied
___ tender   ___ moody, volatile
___ good listener   ___ angry
___ steady   ___ disrespectful
___ difficult   ___ top priority
___ unpredictable   ___ great relationship
___ friend   ___ gave time

Now, go back through the list and put an "x" next to the same descriptions that capture ways your husband treats you. You can see that many husbands end up treating their wives just as their fathers treated their mothers.

SEVEN LESSONS WE LEARN FROM DAD

What your husband knows about manhood, he learned from his dad. True enough, teachers, preachers, coaches, and peers form the supporting cast, but the single greatest influence on the manhood of a boy is his dad.

Our community has been gripped by the trial of an eighteen-year-old boy who savagely murdered a four-year-old girl. He comes from a horribly broken family. During months of pretrial hearings and finally the trial, the boy showed no emotion. But when his father entered the courtroom, his head dropped, he shut his eyes, and his jaw quivered. When his father testified, he teetered on the brink of tears.

There are seven special lessons that every dad, consciously or subconsciously, wants to pass on as a heritage to his son. I know my dad did.

Lesson 1: What it Means to be a Man

I remember the masculinity of my father. My father was a man's man. I learned how to be a man by watching him, by imitating what he would model, by mimicking him, by pretending I was him.

My dad was my hero. My dad couldn't do anything wrong. Later, of course, I learned my dad had weaknesses just like everyone else, but my dad was special. Proverbs 17:6 puts it this way: "The glory of children is their father" (NKJV).

Teachers, preachers, coaches, and peers form the supporting cast, but the single greatest influence on the manhood of a boy is his dad.

When the kids in the neighborhood argued back and forth, "My dad can beat up your dad.... My dad's stronger than your dad.... My dad's better than your dad," I really believed my dad *was* better than your dad! Unless your husband's father gave him reason to think otherwise, he feels the same way about his dad.

As I entered the seventh grade, we moved to five acres in the country. We spent the next several years fixing the place up. I say "we" because Dad put us to work. Yet, somehow he made us four boys feel like we were his partners, not just his slave labor.

I became a man at my father's feet. He showed me what it meant to be a "Morley man." He mentored me to work hard. He modeled a positive approach to life. He exhorted me to never give up my dream. He disciplined me to keep my promises. He tutored me to always tell the truth. He trained me how to handle money.

Lesson 2: How to Treat a Woman

Tim's parents are still living, still married after forty-eight years, and have a wonderful relationship with each other.

Tim said, "I learned how to treat a lady by watching the way my dad was with my mom—even though I was too young to know it at the time! Many, perhaps most, of the expectations I have of my wife—at least before my wife let me know what my expectations ought to be!—were formed as I watched the way my father moved around, looked at, talked to, and responded to his wife. Initially with my wife, I merely copied what I saw my dad do."

Many, perhaps most, of the expectations I have of my wife were formed as I watched the way my father moved around, looked at, talked to, and responded to his wife. Initially with my wife, I merely copied what I saw my dad do.

Husbands learn how to treat their wives principally from observing their fathers. However, husbands also learn by how their fathers let them treat their own mothers, as the following example illustrates.

When Duane first took Kathy, now his wife, to meet his family, he could tell his parents fell in love with Kathy at first sight, and she with them. However, as he was taking Kathy home later that evening she startled him by saying, "Duane, did you know that you were speaking disrespectfully to your mother tonight?"

"What are you talking about?" he asked. She explained what she meant. He stopped, and that was the end of it. But how did it happen at all?

Duane's father had always treated his mother with the greatest respect, but for some reason he let Duane get away with talking back to his mother and making cutting remarks. It was simply a blind spot for his dad and, consequently and inevitably, for Duane.

Your husband learned how to treat you as a "lady"—or not—from his dad.

Lesson 3: A Strong Work Ethic

My dad taught me how to provide for my own family. I learned the importance of hard work at my father's workbench.

Dad worked for and later owned an air-conditioning sales and service company. One summer he asked me if I would like to be his "helper."

"Sure, Dad!" I said. I was so excited to be with my dad. He further astonished me by offering to pay me $1.00 an hour for something I would happily have done for free just to be with him!

For the next several summers I was my dad's "attic rat." He had me wriggle around in hot, steamy crawl spaces to help rig duct work for the air-conditioning systems he installed.

By his example he showed me the importance of diligence, industry, and sticking with it. I appreciate that so much. His deliberate, steady application of mind and body to a problem always paid off. I knew that was the way to go.

Whatever value your husband places on hard work, he learned most of it from his dad.

Lesson 4: Common Sense

David said, "I remember all the little practical things my father imparted to me about the routine of daily living. My dad was not a big talker, but he would regularly splice in choice tidbits about how to live in a practical way. He never offered long-winded sermons, but his one-sentence homilies packed a punch.

"My dad has unusual common sense," he continued. "He sees everything from a practical point of view. He mentored me in the art of putting things in their proper perspective."

Ever wonder where that level-headed, big-picture, common-sense, practical wisdom that from time to time amazes you about your husband came from? Thank his dad.

Lesson 5: Value System

Then there are the larger lessons of right from wrong.

Michael volunteered, "I recall so well the value system we learned around the dinner table as my father and mother would talk through the issues that would influence our lives. The value of education. The value of doing the right thing by other people. The importance of faith. The role of hopes and dreams. The dignity of people.

"I never had a clue about the prejudice of some small-minded people against minorities until long after I had left home. It never occurred to us to make a racial slur in our family. I was shocked the first time I heard racial hatred, because it just wasn't the value I picked up in my house. Dad would have gone ballistic if one of us had used a racial slur in our home. He would have knocked us into next Sunday!"

Good parenting provides no guarantee our children will turn out right, but bad parenting often means they will turn out wrong.

You can trace the roots of your husband's value system back to his father's take on the world.

Lesson 6: Integrity

During those summers when I worked with my dad he would occasionally have a dispute with someone. Yet, I can never remember my dad speaking an ill word about anyone.

My dad never cheated anybody. He never lied. He always took the hard road but the high road. He always told the truth. He was scrupulous in the details. He gave me that moral mooring, that foundation, of integrity.

Good parenting provides no guarantee our children will turn out right, but bad parenting often means they will turn out wrong. If your husband has integrity, he most likely caught it from his dad.

Lesson 7: Spiritual Heritage

John said, "Though I did not come to faith until I was in my mid-twenties, I must thank my dad for the lessons of a spiritual heritage. My parents made sure I was involved every time our church offered youth activities. They put me in youth group, Sunday school, church, confirmation classes—you name it. I didn't understand much at the time, but later I realized a foundation had been formed."

A high school student was walking down the hall to the bedroom. The door to the master bedroom was open, though the lights were out. This teenager's father was kneeling next to his bed in prayer. Ten minutes later when the student went back up the hallway to the family room the father was still praying. This teenager turned adult said, "The visual image of my father praying for so long is forever etched on my mind. It has strongly influenced the way I handle my own spiritual life."

Some fathers mentor their children spiritually through informal homilies. Others read bedtime Bible stories. Perhaps only a few actually plan their children's spiritual education with intentionality, like family devotions. Yet, whatever fathers will do seems to get through.

A FATHER'S LOVE

*I*n the middle of my senior year I quit high school and joined the army. Obviously, I had some issues I was struggling over.

From that point on I didn't have much relationship with my father. Something was severed in the middle of that senior year.

After returning to town I finished high school and college, married, came to Christian faith, and began to mature. As the years peeled off the calendar I began to long for a deeper relationship with my dad, but I didn't know what to do about it.

One year in my early thirties I invited my dad to lunch on his birthday, and it has become an annual custom. One day, a few years after we started this new tradition, we left the cash register and were walking to our cars. For some still unknown reason I said, "Here, Dad. Let me give you a hug."

Before I had time to think about what I had just said, we embraced. I put my arms around my father, and my father put his arms around me. He squeezed so tight it felt like a grizzly bear had grabbed hold of me! Then, he let out a long, deep, primordial sounding groan. "Mmmmmmmm...." It must have lasted thirty seconds.

All I could think of was the deeply buried pain of not having a father of his own, of never having a father of his own to mimic, of never having had a father tussle his hair, of never hearing a father's instruction about the ways of life ... and of the missed years we had not hugged.

At the end of those thirty infinite seconds, warm, salty tears rolled down both of our cheeks. He looked at me, and I looked at him.

I said, "I love you, Dad."

He said, "I love you, too," and then we left, souls cleansed.

Frankly, I'm not sure anyone can adequately explain what happened in those precious moments. A century of sorrows boiled to the surface in one brief instant. The intangible pain of what could have been melted away. A taste of the shimmering glory of paradise broke upon us. The gracious hand of

God broke down a wall. A reconciliation took place. It was a spiritual healing of unspeakable joy.

It's interesting. That single moment became a turning point in our family. Ever since, we have become a family of huggers and lovers. And not just Dad and me—everyone! At first it almost seemed ridiculous.

I would call my brother on the phone. (I'm making this up, but barely.) As we would finish the call he would say, "I love you, Pat."

Then I would say, "I love you, too."

Then he would say, "Well, I love you more than you love me."

"No you don't. I love you more than you love me!"

"That's ridiculous! I said it first!"

Then I would say, "Well, I don't care what you say. I love you more!" then quickly hang up to get in the last word.

If your husband's father didn't verbally and physically express his love for your husband, you can be sure he hungers for it (whether he can articulate it or not).

Our family certainly hugged before that fateful luncheon, but incidentally. Now, hugging is a lifestyle! We always greet each other, coming or going, with hugs and embraces and verbal expressions of love. It's a great life!

I don't mean to suggest this experience can be reproduced by every man. It wouldn't be fair to raise expectations so high. Yet, many men remain distant from their fathers, even unreconciled. Some men may want to give it a try.

No father is perfect. Often fathers leave love unsaid and undone. If your husband's father didn't verbally and physically express his love for your husband, you can be sure he hungers for it (whether he can articulate it or not).

A FATHER'S APPROVAL

In addition to verbal and physical expressions of love, the other important need that often goes unmet by imperfect fathers is his son's need to hear that his dad is proud of him.

One of Florida's leading businessmen told me the story about his installation as an elder in his church. His father had long been an elder there, and that's what motivated him to seek the office. Then he said, "As I was standing there after we were installed, my father came over, put his hand on my shoulder and said, 'Son, I'm proud of you.'"

Every man I know wants to hear his dad say, "I'm proud of you, son."

As he recounted the story, tears began to flow down his sixty-five-year-old face. He added, "Even though I was a grown man, that was the first time I had ever heard my dad say that he was proud of me."

Every man I know wants to hear his dad say, "I'm proud of you, son." Not every son hears it. Larry said one day, "No matter what I did I could never please my father." Larry's dad has been dead now for several years. Yet, the approval his father withheld still motivates Larry to make his dad proud.

So many things turn on the relationship between a father and his son. Can you think of any unresolved issues between your husband and his father?

HOW YOU CAN HELP YOUR HUSBAND

Recently I shared with a man the story of how my father and I hugged and said, "I love you" to each other. Moved, he decided to try the same thing with his dad. In fact, they already had a time together scheduled.

A week later he said to me, "It was unbelievable! I'm forty, but my father has never once expressed any affection toward me physically or verbally. So, I just walked over to him, gave him a bear hug, and said, 'Dad, I love you.' He was dazed! He rocked back, speechless. I felt the weight of the world lift from my shoulders. I think he really appreciated it. I really do love him."

If your husband has any unresolved issues with his father that have caused pain for him, you, or your children, encourage him to seek peace and reconciliation. Perhaps you could suggest he read "A Thought for Husbands," which follows. He may even want to read the entire chapter.

How we remember "dad" forms the silent motivator for much of our behavior.

Be gentle. While on one hand he may long to go and seek his dad's approval, on the other hand a deep bitterness, or fear of being hurt again, often restrains him from trying. Yet, the heart of Christ is forgiveness and reconciliation. Encourage him. If he gives it a try and he fails, he will be no worse off than he is now. But my experience is that fathers want this as much as their sons.

If your husband's father was not a good role model for fathering, encourage your husband to separate his view of God, his perfect heavenly Father, from his view of his mistake-prone earthly father. Encourage him to study the character and attributes of God his Father and not to attribute to God the mistakes of his own dad.

A THOUGHT FOR HUSBANDS

*F*or years a woman expressed frustration over the way her husband demanded that she wait on him hand and foot.

Everything fell into place when they spent a long weekend with his parents. She saw that her husband treated her exactly like his father treated his mother.

Each and every interaction we men had with our fathers was a thread woven into the fabric of the men we are today. Whether good or bad or none at all, our relationship with our dads hums in the background like the gigantic force field of a powerful electromagnet that quietly, or loudly, draws us in its direction. How we remember "dad" forms the silent motivator for much of our behavior.

You and I learned, or didn't learn, the most basic lessons of life from our fathers: What it means to be a man, how to treat a woman, a work ethic, common sense, a value system, integrity, and a spiritual heritage.

How we view our earthly father often molds how we view God, our heavenly Father. Some fathers love their sons unconditionally, but others are harsh and demanding. It's unfortunate. Some men have such horrible thoughts when they hear the word "father" that they find it difficult to relate to God.

The more I have learned to revere God, the more I see him as the Perfect Parent.

God is an altogether perfect parent, unlike frail fathers of flesh and bone. If you've been let down by your earthly father, don't hold it against your heavenly Father. Take the initiative to gain a biblical view of what it means to have a heavenly Father. To grasp this is to find the freedom to forgive, the knowledge to be more like God in your own fathering, and the power to truly love.

Personally, the study of the attributes and character of God has opened up a richness in my spiritual life that has taken me to depths and heights of understanding I never imagined possible. The more I have learned to revere God, the more I see him as the Perfect Parent.

We each long to hear those liberating, uplifting words, "Son, I'm proud of you." They may never come from our earthly father. Whether they do or not, examine how your relationship with your father is shaping your relationship with your wife, both positively and negatively, by answering the following questions:

1. In what ways have you become like your own father? Give an example. In what ways are you different? Give an example.

2. Describe the heritage your father passed along to you using no more than five words. What is the heritage you are passing along to your own kids? To what extent are you repeating the good things your father instilled? Give an example. To what extent are you repeating the mistakes and sins of your father? Give an example.

3. No dad is perfect. In the wake of his own pressures your father may have left a trail of broken relationships and hurt feelings. If you were hurt by your father, is it time to forgive and move on and break the cycle of past mistakes? Tell him you love him. Give him a hug. Be the initiator in the relationship. If this is not possible, how can looking to your heavenly Father fill in the gaps left by your earthly father?

4. Assignment: By tomorrow evening tell your wife two things about your father—one good and one not so good—that you believe still influence your behavior today. If you need to apologize to her for something, go ahead and do it. Now, bury it, and move on. Look to God your true Father.

Two ❧

Significance
What Is It That Your Husband Wants?

A salesman works tirelessly for twelve hours a day, six days a week, for eight weeks to win a sales contest so he can stand for fifteen seconds on top of a dais before his peers to receive a plaque, which he will hang on his wall where it gathers dust. When he changes companies he will take his plaque with him and, though he will never hang it up again, neither will he throw it away.

What is the need that this salesmen is trying to satisfy?

When I was an aspiring young businessman I came home from work one day, closed the garage door, walked over to the wall, and for several minutes kicked it with the sole of my shoe. I was trying to somehow purge the inner frustration of finding success only to feel like it didn't really matter.

Another day, before work, I paced back and forth in front of my wife, Patsy, ranting and raving, trying to expel the angst chewing away at my gut. As I glanced over at her I saw large tears rolling down her cheeks. She wasn't sobbing. She was just sitting there trying to take it "like a man." I tried to look away, but could not. I was transfixed. After she held my gaze for a brief eternity she asked, "Pat, is there anything about me that you like?"

Every husband seeks the same ultimate thing: He wants to experience joy in his life.

As those white hot words lanced my festered soul I fell back in shock, wandered off to my office, stared out the window, and thought to myself, "What happened to you, Morley? You wanted your life to count—to make a difference! You wanted your life to have an impact, to make a contribution, to have meaning and purpose, to do something, to be somebody, to have significance. But you're just a nobody headed nowhere." And it was true.

What unmet need could make a man so desperate that he would pound a wall and say things to his wife that a man should never say?

WHAT IS IT THAT MEN WANT?

Blaise Pascal wrote, "All men seek happiness. This is without exception.... This is the motive of every action of every man, even of those who hang themselves."[1]

Victor Frankl, survivor of four Nazi concentration camps, said, "Man's search for meaning is the primary motivation in his life."[2] This is another way of saying the same thing as Pascal.

Every husband seeks the same ultimate thing: He wants to experience joy in his life. He may call it by many names—happiness, success, contentment, fulfillment, joy, pleasure, enjoyment, delight, significance, purpose, and meaning. These ideas weave together into a single cloth.

The question is, "How does this pleasure, this fulfillment, this joy come to a man?" A man's life consists of his *relation-*

ships and his *tasks*. Of utmost importance to men are their relationships with
God, their wives, and their children.

A MAN'S GREATEST NEED

*A*fter his relationship with God and his
family, what gets your husband out of
bed in the morning?... What makes him
happy?... How is he fulfilled?

At the core of every man boils an intense desire "to do," to master his world, to shape the course of events.

Besides a second cup of coffee, your
husband longs for his life to count, to
matter. At the core of every man boils an intense desire "to
do," to master his world, to shape the course of events. Your
husband is made for the task. Yet, not merely task for task's
sake, but task with meaning.

Listen between the lines to the yearnings from responses to
a survey in which we asked men to complete this sentence:
"My greatest need in general is _____."

- To live my life with purpose
- To make a difference
- To experience a feeling of worth
- To find more meaningful employment
- To have value in life
- To feel I am contributing to life
- To be used by Jesus every day
- To grow and develop every day
- To stay focused on God's plan for my life
- To live the rest of my life for God's will

In the heart of every man burns an intense desire to lead a
more significant life. A man's most innate need is his need to
be significant—to find meaning and purpose to life, to make
a difference, to accomplish something with his life.

In the movie *Chariots of Fire*, Eric Liddell plans to run for an Olympic gold medal. But his sister Jenny wants him to return to the mission field in China. In a famous scene on the Scottish highlands, Eric holds Jenny by her shoulders and says, "Jenny, Jenny, I know that God has made me for a purpose, for China. But he has also made me fast, and when I run I feel God's pleasure."

A man's most innate need is his need to be significant— to find meaning and purpose to life, to make a difference, to accomplish something with his life.

Your husband "feels God's pleasure" when he is using his natural abilities, his developed competencies, and his spiritual gifts. He thrives when consumed in a useful cause.

Men express it in different ways: "I want my life to count, to make a difference, to have an impact, to be filled with meaning, to have purpose, to make a contribution, to do something important with my life, to live a life of significance."

He doesn't want to become just another notch on the belt of history. He doesn't want to be a shooting star that burned out halfway across the sky one night.

This compelling desire animates not just top managers but all men. Michael Novak, in *Business as a Calling*, says,

> Being a middle manager is not primarily a way station on the way to the top. Probably everyone wants at first to test themselves against that possibility; but, realistically, most middle managers expect ... to remain middle managers until retirement. Middle management, many know early, is their calling. They want to be super good at it. They want to make a contribution. Most of

all, they need to know in their own minds that they have done so.[3]

The ambition to conquer, achieve, and excel has driven men ever since that first Neanderthal poked his head out of his cozy cave and wondered what it would be like to harness a flashing bolt of lightning or scoop out a pool next to his cave to collect the rains.

Today George Mallory's frozen body is encased in an icy grave somewhere within a stone's throw of Everest's summit. Once asked why he wanted to conquer the world's tallest temptation, George Mallory gave that famous, poetic-but-haunting response, "Because it is there." Men don't need any further explanation to understand what Mallory meant.

HOW MEN GO ABOUT SATISFYING THEIR GREATEST NEED

How do men go about satisfying this need to be significant? One man I know thinks he will find significance by becoming financially independent. The desire to make enough money to be secure consumes every waking moment. Yet, he could easily retire today and never have to work again.

Another man I know is driven to build a large, highly respected business. The hope for prestige and respect from business success silently motivates his actions. He wants to be "somebody." He has a gross revenue goal in mind that will signify success to him.

A man said, "To me, I will achieve significance when I become the chief financial officer of a medium-sized company."

Another man dedicates himself to developing a reputation as a public speaker. He puts in hours of practice on his delivery and studies other speakers for clues to achieve excellence.

One man I know finds his significance by devoting himself to raising his children. They are all married now, and he has four

A man will find "meanings" in many areas of life. However, he will not be truly happy unless he finds meaning and purpose in his work.

of the most outstanding young people in their twenties you will ever meet.

Yet another man finds his meaning and purpose by throwing himself into the work of his church. He is a deacon, a Sunday school teacher, and an usher. Whenever the doors open, he is there.

In short, to find significance men pursue excellence or competence in some field, whether carpentry or computers, plumbing or public accounting.

A man will find "meanings" in many areas of life: with his God, his wife, his children, his work, the worthwhile use of his gifts and abilities. However, a man will not be truly happy unless he finds meaning and purpose in his work.

THE DIFFERENCE IN MEN

Of these things we can be sure: Men are made for the task; men are going to pursue significance; men are going to climb mountains. The difference in men, however, is in how they go about satisfying their need to be significant.

The issue is not so much *what* men actually do, but *why* they do what they do. What is the motive behind the effort? Men can pursue a life of significance in an *appropriate* or an *inappropriate* way.

If a man's motive is for people to think he is wonderful or great—because he has status, power, money, good looks, a great job, writes successful books, speaks well, has super kids, is righteous, hangs with the "right" people, or whatever—then he is pursuing significance in a way that exalts self.

If, on the other hand, a man does what he does out of the overflow of his personal relationship with Jesus, then everything proceeds from gratitude for what God has already done and is doing in him. He is not motivated by some elusive goal that he (erroneously) thinks will satisfy him.

Let's consider two men, Bob and Jim, both selling life insurance. Bob, father of three boys, wants to lead a life of significance, but as a *response* to what he understands God has already done for him through Christ. He wants to do something with his life not to *gain* significance, but because he realizes that he has already been made significant by God.

When he ponders all that God has done and is doing for him, he finds his forty-two-year-old heart filling up with gratitude for God's grace. His work is his calling, he enjoys good health, and his marriage is rock solid. He has lost two major accounts recently, but Bob keeps the faith.

Out of overflow of his gratitude for God's blessings, he wants to "do" something as an expression of his gratitude to God.

So, out of overflow of his gratitude for God's blessings, he wants to "do" something as an expression of his gratitude to God. He is pursuing his significance in an appropriate way. He feels grateful for his abilities and operates in his *comfort zone*.

Hard-charging Jim, on the other hand, always strives to attain some insatiable goal, which he erroneously thinks will satisfy him. He thinks, "If I could just reach *this* goal or *that* goal, *then* I would be satisfied." He believes that if he could just make this much money, get that job, live in a particular neighborhood, earn the right promotion, get his picture in the paper, or join the right country club, *then* he would be significant.

Jim wants to lead a life of significance, but he always thinks of it as something yet unattained. For him it is elusive, always just beyond his grasp. No matter how much he accomplishes he is not fulfilled. In his unfulfilling search for significance he overcommits himself to do more and more until he winds up in a *pressure zone* weighed down by debts and duties.

Bob pursues significance in an appropriate way, out of the overflow of gratitude for what God has already done. Jim pursues significance in an inappropriate way, hoping that one day he will have enough money, do enough good deeds, and receive enough recognition from his peers to satisfy the yearning he feels for meaning and purpose.

FINDING HAPPINESS AND MEANING

Your husband's greatest yearning is to feel as though his life has mattered. Because men are wired to love their work, the vocations they love often consume them.

Because men are wired to love their work, the vocations they love often consume them.

Ultimately, however, to achieve a success that matters your husband must balance a number of priorities against his vocation. If your husband is walking with God he knows what he needs to do, but occasionally he does need to be reminded.

The men interviewed for this book understand what their priorities should be. They want their wives to know they know. How well husbands apply them, of course, is another matter—one that will occupy much of this book. Let's briefly introduce the top priorities husbands must manage to find true significance and happiness.

His Lord

Ben, a confirmed workaholic, climbed rapidly through the ranks of his public accounting firm. As an audit partner he would leave his family and be on the road for weeks at a time. His work was the main source of meaning in his life.

Eventually, the work pace led to bad health, and he was forced to take early retirement at the age of fifty-two. In the weeks, then months, and eventually years following his retirement, no one from his office ever gave him a call to see how he was doing.

He became bitter that he had given his best years to people who didn't even care enough to call and see how he was adjusting. He began a part-time accounting practice out of his home to keep from going crazy. One day Ben finished an audit, walked into the bathroom, had a heart attack and slumped to the tile floor where he died alone, a bitter, broken, friendless man.

In the book of Ecclesiastes Solomon penned some of the most exquisite wisdom literature ever conceived. The message of Ecclesiastes is clear: Apart from God life has no meaning.

Yet even Solomon lived not the wisdom but the folly of Ecclesiastes. He got his priorities mixed up. He followed other gods. After a life of accomplishment the Bible reports, "As Solomon grew old, his wives turned his heart after other gods, and his heart was not fully devoted to the LORD his God" (1 Kings 11:4). It seems that Solomon died a bitter, broken man.

As your husbands, we cannot find lasting significance apart from God.

His Wife

A lawyer took his wife out to dinner and, as they entered the restaurant, he held the door for her. Later he jokingly said to friends, "I was fulfilling my highest degree of utility." He was kidding around, but he was also expressing a profound understanding of how important it is for husbands to honor and respect their wives.

As your husbands, we cannot find lasting significance apart from God.

One man said, "The most important thing I've ever learned is that I must make God my top priority. Then, after God, but before all others, my wife must be my next priority. Now I honor my wife. This has released her to reveal to me a side of her that I had never known. It's been great."

As your husbands we cannot find lasting significance and happiness unless our commitment to love, cherish, and nurture our wives occupies our uppermost thoughts.

His Children

Steve wanted to get into the trucking business. He purchased one truck and began making short hauls around the city. To establish himself he left every morning before the children awakened, and arrived home after they had gone to bed. One night as his wife was putting his three-and-a-half-year-old, Shawn, to bed the boy sat up and asked, "Mommy, where does Daddy live?"

Later that evening, when Steve came home, his wife related the story. At first he chuckled, but then it sobered him. He realized that he was confusing the "means" and the "end." Originally he started the trucking business as a "means" to the "end" of providing for his family and meeting their needs.

Steve realized that somewhere along the line the business had become the "end" and he had unwittingly let his family become the "means." He was using his family to help him accomplish his business goals, instead of using his business to help him accomplish his family goals. He decided to get his priorities back in line. It took two years, but he did it. No amount of success at work can compensate for failure at home.

My wife's cousin is a pastor. When his son married, he joyfully performed the ceremony. He smiled fully at the assembled friends, then said wistfully to no one in particular, "Where did the time go?"

As fathers we cannot find the significance we desire if we don't have enough time for our children. We teach men, "If you don't have enough time for your children, you can be 100 percent certain you are not following God's will for your life." Relationships create responsibilities. Time is everything to a relationship. It's important for us to give time to whom time is due.

His Vocation

I'm sure you have met men socially who seem quite ordinary, yet you have been surprised to learn that professionally they are rather dynamic. A conversation with any man that reaches an awkward lull can be rejuvenated by a question about his work.

Man is a worker. Man is made to work. Men are made for the task. When Marianne turned deathly ill in the movie *Sense and Sensibility*, the unoccupied, gentry classed Colonel Brandon, who loved her deeply, said, "Give me something to do or I shall go mad!"

When my younger brother, Robert, died tragically I went straight from the funeral to work. A secretary from accounting brought some papers to my office and said, "You look pale. Don't you think you should go home?"

"Thanks, but right now this is where I need to be," I answered.

At the core of every man boils an intense desire "to do." As your husbands we will not find lasting purpose and meaning unless we perform fulfilling work.

WHAT MEN WILL SACRIFICE

When King David learned that Bathsheba was pregnant, he schemed to bring her husband, Uriah, back from battle so he would sleep with his wife and take David off the hook. When Uriah appeared, David sent him home. But Uriah slept instead at the entrance to the palace. The next day David called him in and asked, "Why didn't you go home?"

In 2 Samuel 11:11 we find a revealing characteristic of men. In this passage Uriah said, "The ark and Israel and Judah are staying in tents, and my master Joab and my lord's men are camped in the open fields. How could I go to my house to eat and drink and lie with my wife? As surely as you live, I will not do such a thing!"

In other words, "How could I be with my wife when my coworkers need me? How could I think of my personal life when my fellow employees are working overtime?"

If a man has to make a sacrifice somewhere, usually the last thing he will sacrifice is his job.

What, pray tell, was Uriah talking about? The issue is this: What will a man make a sacrifice for, and what will he sacrifice?

First, what will a man make a sacrifice for? If a man has to make a sacrifice somewhere, usually the last thing he will sacrifice is his job. Here is an axiom many men live by: *The better the man, the more loyal he is to his job.*

Second, what will men sacrifice if not their job? Generally, a man will sacrifice family before vocation. He will tend to give his work priority over family. Why is that? I think most men have wrongly defined what it means to be a provider. They think of "providing" primarily as a financial responsibility—the physical and material needs of money, shelter, food, clothing, car insurance, education, and so on.

Some husbands, of course, need to rethink the term "provider." A provider meets the needs of the family, whatever they may be—material, physical, emotional, or spiritual.

Just out of curiosity, what would your husband make a sacrifice for, and what would he sacrifice?

YOUR HUSBAND

Which of the following descriptions best fits your husband?

Your husband has been pursuing significance in a right way. He has found his calling. He works and serves out of the gratitude for all that God has already done for him. He manages all of his priorities. Thank God for this man.

Your husband has been pursuing significance in a wrong way. His motives are wrong. He's confused. He wants to stand on a platform to receive an honor that he erroneously thinks will make him happy. He has God-given ability, but he has been living for his own motives. Encourage this man to think more deeply about his life, perhaps by reading this chapter.

Your husband has given up. He wanted to find significance once, but that was a long time ago. Perhaps he was told by his father, "You'll never amount to anything. You're stupid." When he hears a young man speak of his dreams he thinks, "I had a dream once. It died when nobody cared." Your unconditional love, support, and respect can help heal his wounds.

Your husband is still seeking. He has not yet found what he is looking for, but he hasn't given up. He may be in the wrong job. Perhaps you should encourage him to find a job he can love. What is the thing that will make him "feel God's pleasure"?

HOW YOU CAN HELP YOUR HUSBAND

Everyone has a greatest need. Wives have a greatest need. Children have a greatest need. Husbands have a greatest need.

Wives, think for a moment how intensely you feel about your greatest need. It may be the need for intimacy with your husband or for security. Whatever it is, your husband feels just as intensely about his greatest need as you do about yours. He is motivated by his greatest need just as you are motivated by yours. What is the need that animates your husband?

Pray for your husband—that he will find a life of significance, purpose, and meaning.

Ultimately, we all—husbands, wives, and children alike—want to be happy, fulfilled, and content. Send your husband positive signals that you understand his greatest need, you appreciate it, and you want to be his partner in helping him satisfy it. This will go miles to encourage him.

Anything we feel passionate about we can also overdo. In the game of life your husband will most definitely get carried away on occasion with his work or the other interest where he "feels God's pleasure." When he does, without necessarily meaning to, he will neglect other priorities. Remind him gently. He really does want to do the right thing. And pray for him—that he will find a life of significance, purpose, and meaning.

A THOUGHT FOR HUSBANDS

Pounding in the breast of every man is an intense desire to lead a more significant life. A man's most innate need is his need to be significant—to find meaning and purpose in life, to make a difference, to accomplish something with his life.

All men want to lead a life of significance. In fact, how we each pursue this significance is what really differentiates one man from the next.

We can pursue significance in appropriate and inappropriate ways. The difference is not so much in what we do, but why we do it—our motives. Do you think you have been pursuing significance in a right way? To consider this more deeply you may want to read this entire chapter.

Ultimately, to achieve a success that really matters, we each must balance our desire for vocational success against our other priorities, namely God, our wives, and our children.

Three ❧

Obstacles
What's Troubling Your Husband?

$\mathcal{R}$ecently a wife told me she was having difficulty figuring out how to offer support to her husband. He loves his work. Occasionally, for stretches of months at a time, he will work twelve hours a day. Then suddenly his mood will swing, and he will mope around for months. "What is it that you want?" she asks him. He cannot articulate an answer.

How can a man get exactly what he wanted and not be happy?

To me she said, "I can chart these cycles on paper. They're completely predictable. I just don't know what to do for him any-more. He is extremely successful. He has the job he always wanted. We have a beautiful home and two lovely children. What's his problem?"

How can a man get exactly what he wanted and not be happy? This is one of the questions we'll explore in this chapter.

OBSERVATIONS ABOUT HOW MEN ARE DOING

$\mathcal{M}$any men today are hurting. Their careers aren't turning out the way they planned or, what's sometimes worse, they *are*.

For the most part, their marriages are not working the way they're supposed to. Their wives are disappointed in them, romance has been replaced by routine, and communication has dried up. Where once there was friendship, there is truce.

Their kids don't seem appreciative, and they're up to their receding hairlines in financial problems.

If I could make only one observation about men today, it would be that men are tired—mentally, emotionally, physically, and spiritually tired.

If I could make only one observation about men today, it would be that men are tired—mentally, emotionally, physically, and spiritually tired. Weary of life. When I make this observation at our men's seminars it evokes as much response as anything else I say. Many heads nod in agreement while others droop to their chests.

Not only are men tired, they often have a lingering feeling something isn't quite right about their lives. A man and I were talking on a plane about the challenges men face today. He said, "You know, I don't get it. I'm three times as financially successful as my father ever dreamed of being. But I just have this deep, nagging doubt that somehow I've missed the point."

Many times men's lives are not turning out the way they planned. To Johnny Oates, general manager of the Texas Rangers baseball team, the most important thing in life was big league baseball.

He said, "Baseball took most of my time. Then the press. Then the fans. My wife and kids were at the bottom half of the list. The first thing I thought about every morning was what lineup I would use. Who would hit fifth? Who was hurt? If the team was going bad, what could I do."[1]

Johnny said, "I had deserted my family emotionally, phys-ically, and spiritually for fifteen years. I took a mistress. My mistress was baseball."

One day his wife and daughter were driving to watch one of his games. They checked into a motel for the night. His wife woke up in the middle of the night with a panic attack. His daughter tried to help her mom, but things got worse. Finally, his daughter said, "Mom, I'm calling Dad."

His wife answered, "Honey, don't you know? Baseball doesn't stop even for death."

Johnny said, "That was my wake-up call. I skipped the next five games to be at home while Gloria was recovering. I had my priorities reversed. Now we're in a process of healing things."

COMING UNGLUED AND NOBODY CARES

*M*any husbands strive to put a good face on things at the same time their lives are coming unglued. Once I struck up a new business relationship with a man that required me to call him about every six months to put our deal together.

The first time I called him I said, "Hi, Tom, how are you doing?"

"Perfect! Just perfect!" he said.

I thought to myself, *Whatever you say*, and we went ahead and talked business.

Six months later I called again, asking, "Hi, Tom, how are you doing?"

"Perfect! Pat, I'm just perfect!"

Yea, right. Sure you are, I thought, and I finished up the second leg of our transaction. But I started thinking about his canned responses.

After another six months I rang him up to do the final leg of our business deal. "Hi, Tom, this is Pat. How are you doing?"

"Perfect! I'm just perfect!"

Because I had been thinking about our previous superficial exchanges I said, "Tom, I don't think you understand the question I'm asking you. I'm not just asking, 'How are you doing?' I'm interested in how are you *really* doing?"

He said, "Oh," which was followed by a pregnant, five-second pause. *One thousand, two thousand, three thousand, four thousand, five thousand …*

"Well, okay," he said, and then Tom launched into a thirty-minute monologue—never came up for air one time, not once!—in which he described one of the most agonizing, tortured kinds of business problems that any man could ever be expected to endure. What's most interesting about this is that he had been going through this jawbreaking problem all the months we had been speaking on the phone: "Perfect, just perfect."[2]

Often it just doesn't seem to men as if anyone really cares. Something akin to the just mentioned scene repeats itself every day in the lives of most men. Men don't tell others how they are *really* doing because they don't think anyone will really want an answer. In truth, most people don't. Those people are up to their eyebrows with problems of their own.

For many men, managing their lives has become like trying to tie two pieces of string together that are not quite long enough. They are long enough to touch, long enough to manipulate, and long enough to create hope that they can be tied together, but they simply are not long enough to tie the knot. Close, but not close enough.[3]

The result? A pervasive lack of contentment stalks them. As Thoreau said, "The mass of men lead lives of quiet desperation." They often find themselves frustrated, discouraged, disillusioned, confused, afraid of the future, lonely, and riddled with guilt over poor decisions they have made. They are restless. They are wondering, "Is this all there is?" They're thinking, "There must be more to life—there's got to be."

"SUCCESS SICKNESS"

*L*ee Atwater had two goals: To manage a winning presidential campaign and become the head of the Republican Party. He managed George Bush's successful 1988 campaign and soon thereafter was appointed chairman of the Republicans.

In March 1990 Atwater was diagnosed with an inoperable brain tumor. Before his death Atwater—who began writing apology notes to political enemies—told columnist Cal Thomas, "I have found Jesus Christ. It's that simple. He's made a difference, and I'm glad I've found him while there's still time." The month Atwater, eaten up with cancer, turned forty he said,

> The 80s were about acquiring—acquiring wealth, power, prestige. I know. I acquired more wealth, power and prestige than most. But you can acquire all you want and still feel empty. What power wouldn't I trade for a little more time with my family? What price wouldn't I pay for an evening with friends? It took a deadly illness to put me eye to eye with that truth, but it is a truth that the country, caught up in its ruthless ambitions and moral decay, can learn on my dime. I don't know who will lead us through the 90s but they must be made to speak to this spiritual vacuum at the heart of American society, this tumor of the soul.

Men in our generation often have a tumor on their soul we might term "success sickness." "Success sickness" is the disease of always wanting more, and never being satisfied when we get it. It is the intangible pain of not achieving goals that should have never been set or achieving them only to find out they didn't really matter. We are the nation that weeps over winning only silver medals.

The greatest problem we see is not that husbands are failing to achieve their goals. They are achieving them. The problem is that they are the wrong goals. In fact, we could say that failure means to succeed in a way that doesn't really matter.

The unhappy result is that many husbands today are struggling with problems that success can't solve. They are not satisfied by what William James called the "bitch goddess of success." As Michael Novak points out, "The aftertaste of affluence is boredom."[4]

Many husbands today are struggling with problems that success can't solve.

No man sets out to fail on purpose. No husband wakes up in the morning and thinks to himself, *I think I'll see how I can neglect my wife today.* Yet every day many men make decisions that slowly, over time, like water tapping on a rock, ruin their lives.

Let's discuss three viruses in particular that infect men with "success sickness."

VIRUS #1: THE RAT RACE

𝒫icture this: Husbands, lots of husbands, men under pressure, zooming down the fast lanes of life, straining to keep pace. Some are oblivious to what they're doing. Some are starting to wonder about it. Others are weary. Still others have "hit the wall."

We have created a culture that requires more energy than men have to give. Sometimes we call it the rat race.

The most highly contagious virus known to the American male is the rat race.

What is the rat race? *The rat race is the endless pursuit of an ever increasing prosperity that ends in frustration rather than contentment.* Francis Schaeffer said that most people have adopted two impoverished values: *personal peace,* not wanting to be bothered with the troubles of others, and *affluence,* a life made up of things, things, and more things.[5] A friend recently told me sheepishly that he has a weakness for golf clubs. He has ten expensive drivers in his closet. Ironically, it's the old beat up one that's his favorite.

On June 8, 1978, a friend of mine stood in a drizzle at Harvard Yard with the other graduating students as Aleksandr Solzhenitsyn delivered the commencement address for Harvard University. It was the custom in those days to boo the speaker, but on this day a hush fell over the audience.

Solzhenitsyn said, "Every citizen has been granted the desired freedom and material goods in such quantity and of such quality as to guarantee in theory the achievement of happiness. . . . In the process, however, one psychological detail has been overlooked: the constant desire to have still more things and a still better life and the struggle to this end imprint many Western faces with worry and even depression, though it is customary to carefully conceal such feelings."[6] In other words, the rat race.

As a result of this virus, many husbands, often who are Christians, have been knocked off balance. In our work with men we regularly meet men who have "prayed a prayer" for salvation, but for the last five, ten, fifteen, twenty, or more years they have been living by their own ideas. They have built on the foundation of their own best thinking. They read the Bible for comfort, but the *Wall Street Journal* for direction.

In the process of pursuing their career goals many men neglect their wives emotionally, and slowly, the two of them grow apart. Taking a cue from dad, kids today often run in their own mini-rat races, and dads sometimes feel left out and unappreciated. Twenty years later it slowly dawns on these men that they gave their best years to careers that promised what they couldn't deliver. In fact, a man will often feel "dumped on" and "used" in his career, a festering bitterness that only further infects the other areas of his life.

Consequently, things are not turning out the way many men planned. Painful questions knife through their thoughts. "What's it all about? How can I be so successful and so unfulfilled at the same time? Is this all there is?" The rat race charges an expensive toll. It will take everything you have to give.

So, how do men get caught up in the rat race? Galatians 5:7 asks the question this way: "You were running a good race. Who cut in on you and kept you from obeying the truth?"

What men believe determines how they live. For many, they have believed and built on the wrong ideas. The problem, Paul noted in Galatians 5:9, is that "A little yeast works through the whole batch of dough."

VIRUS #2: THE UNEXAMINED LIFE

George Bernard Shaw said, "Few people think more than two or three times a year. I have made an international reputation by thinking once or twice a week."

Perhaps the greatest weakness men face at the turn of the twenty-first century is that they tend to lead unexamined lives.

The price of pace is peace.

To lead an unexamined life means to rush from task to busy task, but not call enough time-outs to reflect on life's larger meaning and purpose.

The price of pace is peace. As a man who worked seventy-hour weeks for several years recently told me, "It's been a long, intense run. My life is devoid of any quiet places."

I love technology. Technology is a friend, but this friend also has a dark side.[7] As a man increases his labor-saving devices he also increases his workload and the access other people have to him. The drone of these devices often leaves a man with no place to sit and simply think.

Socrates said, "Know thyself," and Plato wrote, "The unexamined life is not worth living." When men choose to run the gauntlet of the rat race, they barter away their times of reflection and self-examination.

Most men have not carefully chiseled their worldview by a personal search for truth and obedience to God and his Word. Rather, they are drifting. They are not thinking deeply about their lives. Buffeted by the whipping winds of daily pressure, tossed about like a bobbing cork by surging waves of change, men long for the sure-footed sands of simpler days, but with scarcely a clue of how to reach such distant shores.

Only on the anvil of self-examination can God shape a man into the image of his Son.

Lamentations 3:40 exhorts, "Let us examine our ways and test them, and let us return to the LORD." Only on the anvil of self-examination can God shape a man into the image of his Son. "Teach us to number our days aright, that we may gain a heart of wisdom" (Psalm 90:12).

VIRUS #3: CULTURAL CHRISTIANITY

According to surveys by the Billy Graham organization 90 percent of all Christians lead defeated lives.[8] Why is that true for so many husbands?

Something that happened to me is the crux of this book. So let me briefly tell you my story because it is likely your husband's story, too, if only in part.

I vacillated between two sets of heroes. On one hand, I was inspired by great businessmen and athletes who lived for God. I wanted to emulate heroes of the faith like Billy Graham, Mother Teresa, C. S. Lewis, James Dobson, Tom Skinner, and Bill Bright. On the other hand, I secretly aspired to the accomplishments and fortunes of business barons like

Trammel Crow (the number-one real estate developer), Lee Iaccoca, Bill Gates, and Malcolm Forbes.

When I hit the ten-year mark in my spiritual journey I realized something was desperately wrong with my life, but I couldn't put my finger on any one problem. I was an active Christian, reading my Bible and praying regularly, immersed in church life, a vocal witness, and pursuing a moral lifestyle.

Curiously, I was sitting at the top of my career. Materially, I was taken care of wonderfully. Yet, when I would imagine another man thinking how I was blessed, I would want to grab him by the arms, shake him, and scream, "You don't understand! This isn't a blessing, it's a curse!"

There is a God we want and there is a God who is. They are not the same God.

Finally the intangible pain became so strong that I called a "time out" for reflection and self-examination. I spent the next two and a half years staring at my navel.

At first all I could grasp were the thoughts described at the beginning of this chapter:

- I was tired.
- I had a lingering feeling something wasn't quite right about my life.
- My life wasn't turning out the way I had planned.
- I felt like my life was coming unglued.
- I didn't feel like anyone really cared about me, personally.
- I was achieving my goals, but success didn't satisfy.

A couple of years later during a major business crisis, a thought went through my mind as I was sitting in the rubble of my collapsing empire: *There is a God we want and there is a God who is. They are not the same God. The turning point of our lives is when we stop seeking the God we want and start seeking the God who is.*

I realized I had become what we might call a *cultural* Christian. In *The Man in the Mirror* I defined the term this way:

> Cultural Christianity means to seek the God we want instead of the God who is. It is the tendency to be shallow in our understanding of God, wanting Him to be more of a gentle grandfather type who spoils us and lets us have our own way. It is sensing a need for God, but on our own terms. It is wanting the God we have underlined in our Bibles without wanting the rest of Him, too. It is God relative instead of God absolute.[9]

IS YOUR HUSBAND A CULTURAL CHRISTIAN?

When has a man become a cultural Christian? Men become cultural Christians when they seek the God (or gods) they want, and not the God who is.

Men who become cultural Christians read their Bibles with an agenda, if they read them at all. They decide in advance what they want, and then read their Bibles looking for evidence to support the decisions they have already made. In short, they follow the God they are underlining in their Bibles. They create a "fifth gospel."

In many ways they have merely added Jesus to their lives as another interest in an already crowded schedule. They practice a kind of "Spare Tire Christianity"—they keep something in the trunk just in case they have a flat.

They want to have their cake and eat it, too. They have made a plan for their lives. Their credo is, "Plan, then pray." Their lives are shaped more by following the herds of commerce than the footsteps of Christ.

Biblically, these men have let the worries of this life and the deceitfulness of money choke the Word and make it unfruitful (Matthew 13:22); they've let the yeast of culture work through the whole batch of dough (Galatians 5:9); they've done that which is permissible but not beneficial (1 Corinthians 6:12); they're high risk for a great crash because they built on sand and not the rock (Matthew 7:24–27).

Often men like this are what Os Guiness has called "the undiscipled disciple." They have not fully yielded their lives to the lordship of Jesus Christ. They are disciples of Wall Street, not Church Street.

Their worldview tends to be a jumbled concoction of ideas cherrypicked from church, television, *Business Week,* positive thinking seminars, and the Harvard Business School (the technical term for this is *syncretism).*

By default men become cultural Christians when they do not choose to proactively become *biblical* Christians.

Our ministry brings us into contact with countless men speeding down the crowded corridors of commerce, searching for a success that satisfies. Their lives have often become an unrelated string of hollow victories, increasingly frustrating to them as more and more is accomplished.

"Success sickness" is killing your husbands. When we men run in the rat race, lead an unexamined life, and become cultural Christians we must fight off three lethal viruses at the same time. No wonder so many of us feel what Soren Kierkegaard called "the sickness unto death." If we are not careful, it can be a terminal illness.

THE TURNING POINT

If "success sickness" is to reach our goals only to discover they don't really matter, how can men find "success that matters"?

First, a man must reach a turning point. *The turning point of our lives is when we stop seeking the God we want and start seeking the God who is.*

> *Our principal task as men is to come humbly to the foot of the cross of Jesus Christ and there negotiate the terms of a full and complete surrender to his lordship.*

- "Holy, holy, holy is the Lord God Almighty, who was, and is, and is to come" (Revelation 4:8).
- "Then I asked, 'Who are you, Lord?' 'I am Jesus, whom you are persecuting,' the Lord replied" (Act 26:15).
- "For the LORD is the great God, the great King above all gods" (Psalm 95:3).
- "You alone are the LORD" (Nehemiah 9:6).

As Bobby Bowden, Florida State University's football coach, says, "You've got to touch first base. You can't score at home plate if you don't touch first base." "First base" is Jesus Christ. He has given us the promise of eternal life if we "turn."

"Elijah went before the people and said, 'How long will you waver between two opinions?'" (1 Kings 18:21).

God is who he is, and no amount of wanting to recreate him in our imagination is going to have any effect on his unchanging character and nature. Our principal task as men, then, is to come humbly to the foot of the cross of Jesus Christ and there negotiate the terms of a full and complete surrender to the lordship of Jesus Christ.

HOW YOU CAN HELP YOUR HUSBAND

No one knows your husband better than you do. How is he doing? Is he tired? Does he have that lingering feeling something isn't quite right? Does he know what he wants? Does he have a case of "success sickness"? Which of the three viruses that cause "success sickness" does he have—running in the rat race, leading an unexamined life, living as a cultural Christian?

Often, the very things husbands most wish their wives knew about them are the things they most struggle to put into words. Your husband probably couldn't articulate much of what has been said in these last two chapters. Yet that is how many, if not most, men feel inside.

"Success sickness" is the disease of always wanting more, and never being satisfied when we get it.

I know you long to help your husband. And in spite of his occasional rebellion against it, he wants to be helped.

Let me offer two suggestions. First, you are at the beginning of this book. Resist the urge to point things out to him. Rather, keep reading until you have "the bigger picture" of what your husband wishes you knew about him.

Second, pray. Ask God to show you how you can help your husband. As you feel led you might say to your husband, "I'm reading this book about what husbands wish their wives knew about men. I was intrigued by a chapter and I was wondering if you would read it for me and tell me what parts of the chapter, if any, you would want me to know about you?"

A THOUGHT FOR HUSBANDS

*M*any men today are hurting. They are tired of running the rat race. Their energy has been depleted. Their marriages are rocky. Their children are preoccupied. Their finances are in disarray.

Our generation has caught a disease we might term "success sickness." It is the disease of always wanting more, and never being satisfied when we get it.

The greatest problem we face as men isn't that we are failing to achieve our goals. Usually we are achieving them. Often, however, they are the wrong goals. Many times we get what we want only to find out it doesn't really matter.

Life can become like trying to tie two pieces of string together that are not quite long enough. Haunting questions can lurk in our thoughts, "Is this all there is?" We think, "There's got to be more to life than this."

Three viruses in particular infect us with "success sickness": the rat race, leading an unexamined life, and cultural Christianity.

To run the rat race is to endlessly pursue an ever increasing prosperity that ends not in contentment but frustration. To lead an unexamined life means to rush from task to task, but not call enough time-outs to reflect on life's larger meaning and purpose.

Cultural Christianity means to seek the God we want instead of the God who is. It is the tendency to be shallow in our understanding of God, wanting him to be a gentle grandfather who spoils us and lets us have our own way. We become *cultural* Christians when we do not proactively choose to become *biblical* Christians.

When we run the rat race, lead an unexamined life, and become cultural Christians we must fight off three lethal viruses at the same time.

If "success sickness" is to reach our goals only to discover they don't really matter, how can we find "success that matters"? Success that matters is a well-balanced, priority-based success that yields a deep sense of meaning and purpose. It pays attention to all of the key areas of a man's life. It is not based on cultural norms but on the timeless truths of the Bible. Consider these questions:

1. Can you articulate what it is that you want from life?
   (If you would like some suggestions to "lubricate"

your thinking you may want to read this entire chapter).
2. Do you have a case of "success sickness"—even though you may know Christ?
3. Have you been living the life of a cultural Christian?

If yes, have you reached a turning point? *The turning point of our lives is when we stop seeking the God we want and start seeking the God who is.* If so, tell him. Tell him what you want to turn *from*. Tell him what you want to turn *to*. (This process, by the way, is what the Bible calls *repentance*.) If you would like a suggested prayer you may use the following one or paraphrase it in your own words.

Lord Jesus,
I need you in my life right now more than I ever have. I realize that I have been living the life of a cultural Christian. I have been seeking a success that doesn't really matter. As a result, I have contracted "success sickness." I have been seeking the God(s) I have wanted and not the God who is. I have sinned against you, and I am sorry. I ask you to forgive me by your amazing grace. I ask you to take control of my life and make me into the kind of man I know you want me to be—make me into a biblical Christian. Amen.

Four ❧

Pressure

Understanding the Pressure
Your Husband Feels

Pressure. Eighteen-year-old Kerry Strug stares down the runway toward the vault, which in moments will lift her and U.S. women's gymnastics high into the thin air of glory or sink them deep into the murky waters of second-guessing what could have been.

Pressure. The United States Women's Gymnastic Team has never won a team gold medal in the Olympic Games.

Pressure. The Americans hold a slight edge over the relentless Russians in the point standings. All other events completed, the vault stands alone as the single remaining event, the sole arbiter of victory or defeat.

Pressure. Kerry watches as her injured teammate, Dominique, lunges for the apparatus, which twice hurls her down to the mat. Every eye turns anxiously to Kerry who now, as the final competitor, must ace her vault.

Pressure. No one else remains. Kerry stands alone, the last and final hope of Olympic gold. She contemplates her own injuries and puts them out of her mind. She focuses on the vault at the end of the runway. She bursts down the ramp and lurches for the vault. She roughly topples to the ground and sprains her ankle.

Pressure. Kerry hobbles back to the starting line. Second chance. Last chance. She knows the stakes. Gold or goat. Stick this landing or go down in ignominious defeat. Later, it will turn out that her first vault was good enough for gold, but no one knows this at the moment.

The information highway is nothing less than the on-ramp to the rat race.

She explodes off the starting line. She shrugs off every thought of defeat. With sure hands she grips the back of this wriggling gymnastic monster. She catapults herself high into the air. She lands, arms rising up in triumph. She has done it! She has won the gold! And then, staggering, she collapses in pain.

"I felt the pressure," said Kerry, "but it worked to my advantage. It gave me that little extra bit of adrenaline. I knew I could do the vault—I could do it in my sleep. I felt really prepared. I knew I had to do it. I knew I could do it. I just went, and it happened pretty fast."

THE NATURE OF PRESSURE

The young often have an advantage over the old. To their pressures have not been added the weight of dreams that died and hopes hollowed out by disappointment.

Everyone feels pressure. Children feel pressure. Women feel pressure. Men feel pressure. A little pressure, of course, can be a good thing. It can motivate us to do what only we can do, much like it did for Kerry Strug.

Husbands and wives both feel pressures, of course, but at different levels and for different reasons. In this chapter we will help you feel the sources and intensity of your husband's pressures and gain insight into how you can help him be a better pressure manager.

Why is your husband under so much pressure? Why does he push himself so hard? Why does he neglect you and the children? And what, if anything, can a wife do to help her husband with his pressures?

Today we live in an on-line, virtual reality, "real time," technology-driven culture. It is a pressure cooker of change and obsolescence.

The machine gun staccato of change leaves many men reeling—scrambling to keep up. Businesses hustle to stay competitive, and that means tinkering with the existing order (read: downsizing). Because of computers the need for white-collar middle managers shrinks daily like a balloon losing air. The feeling of job stability is gone. A clammy sense of imminent change hangs overhead like the sword of Damocles.

You and the children don't create your husband's anger.

The information highway is nothing less than the on-ramp to the rat race. The paradox of technology is that the more technologically advanced a man becomes, the farther he feels he is falling behind in the race toward progress.

All in all, men today are under a great deal of pressure. And, as anyone knows who has ever played "pressure defense" in sports, men under pressure make mistakes.

Nevertheless, men are practiced at appearing to have things under control, at least at work. This is one reason you see so much "ventilating" at home. You and the children don't create the anger. Rather, you innocently trigger the release of anger that has been building up all day.

FIVE "THORNS" THAT PUT PRESSURE ON YOUR HUSBAND

*M*en must work. Work is a rule of life. The apostle Paul put it this way, "For even when we were with you, we gave you this rule: 'If a man will not work, he shall not eat'" (2 Thessalonians 3:10). Men understand this.

A man must provide for his family. "If anyone does not provide for his relatives, and especially for his immediate family, he has denied the faith and is worse than an unbeliever" (1 Timothy 5:8). Intuitively, men understand this.

Work is a blessing from God. Sometimes, men think work is God's curse. Actually, work was instituted by God before the Fall of Adam. "The LORD God took the man and put him in the Garden of Eden to work it and take care of it" (Genesis 2:15).

Man is made to be a worker, and he cannot find happiness if he is unhappy at work.

Man is made to be a worker, and he cannot find happiness if he is unhappy at work. Often, men don't understand this.

However, work is a blessing made difficult by the Fall. "Because you listened to your wife and ate from the tree about which I commanded you, 'You must not eat of it,' cursed is the ground because of you; through painful toil you will eat of it all the days of your life" (Genesis 3:17). Every man feels this.

Unfortunately, your husband must provide for his family while feeling *the prick of thorns*. Because of the Fall, your husband will feel the prick of thorns every day in his work (you too, of course). They cause a lot of pressure. While every husband is unique in his own way, all men basically are under the same set of pressures. Let's examine five of the sharpest thorns more closely.

TIME

*T*ime pressure is like the thorn that pricked your husband's finger as he innocently reached to pick you a rose. It looked good, but the price was higher that he thought.

Most husbands I meet bemoan that they have too little energy for the demands of modern life. Many have trouble saying no. And it's difficult to balance all of our priorities.

Two years ago I agreed to do a speaking tour to introduce a new book. Since I had never done that before, I unwittingly added the tour to my already busy schedule without subtracting any other commitments.

One day months later an associate and I were on a plane returning from some city and I said to him, "In spite of all the good we are doing, when I look at my calendar my only thought is that I just want to get through it." Not a few men are just trying to get through it.

Every man goes through seasons when he drowns in the ink of his schedule. The real issue is simple: Is it temporary or permanent?

Every man goes through seasons when he drowns in the ink of his schedule. The real issue is simple: Is it temporary or permanent?

In his book *Margin*, medical doctor Richard A. Swenson suggests that we have developed a new disease by overextending ourselves. He calls it "marginless living." Think about your husband as you read what Swenson says.

> Why do so many of us feel like air-traffic controllers out of control? How can the salesman feel so stressed when the car is loaded with extras, the paycheck is bigger than ever, and vacation lasts four weeks a year? How

is it possible that the homemaker is still tired despite the help of the washing machine, clothes dryer, dishwasher, garbage disposal, and vacuum cleaner? If we are so prosperous, why are the therapists' offices so full? If we have ten times more material abundance than our ancestors, why are we not ten times more content and fulfilled?

Something is wrong. People are tired and frazzled. People are anxious and depressed. People don't have the time to heal anymore. There is a psychic instability in our day that prevents peace from implanting itself very firmly in the human spirit. And despite the skeptics, this instability is not the same old nemesis recast in modern life. What we have here is a brand-new disease.... It is the disease of marginless living.

Margin is the amount allowed beyond that which is needed. It is something held in reserve for contingencies or unanticipated situations. Margin is the gap between rest and exhaustion, the space between breathing freely and suffocating. It is the leeway we once had between ourselves and our limits. Margin is the opposite of overload.

If we were equipped with a flashing light to indicate "100 percent full," we could better gauge our capacities. But we don't have such an indicator light, and we don't know when we have overextended until we feel the pain. As a result many people commit to a 120-percent life and wonder why the burden feels so heavy. It is rare to see a life prescheduled to only 80 percent, leaving a margin for responding to the unexpected that God sends our way.[1]

Most men today feel like their time is not their own. In fact, many have so overextended themselves that they have chosen a lifestyle of neglecting their wives and children to meet their other obligations.

An NBC Lifestyle Survey reported on March 9, 1995 found that 59 percent of people said they were "very busy but content" and 10 percent said they were "overloaded." Combined, two out of three people report themselves very busy or overloaded.

What your husband wants you to know is that he hates this, but he can't figure out how to get the noose from around his neck. He feels like his arms are tied with thick ropes of responsibility.

MONEY

Money pressure is like a tangle of blackberry briars that scratched the arms and legs of your husband when he went to the field searching for the family's food. The more he twists to escape, the deeper they dig into him.

The greatest pressure men reported in a survey we completed was financial pressure. Most men feel like they have too much month left at the end of the money!

One husband felt completely frustrated that his wife refused to live by a budget. They have a child in a private high school, a child in a private college, four cars, four car insurance payments, and a plumbing leak!

Finally, after months of talking about it, she agreed that they needed to live by a budget. He's feeling a lot better.

The greatest financial pressure, of course, is "this week." But beyond immediate cash flow pressure, men feel the weight of all their financial duties. Retirement looms larger every year as Social Security seems less secure.

A lump forms in his throat every time the TV flashes one of those ads that shows the cost of a college education to scare us into buying the "right" financial product.

Few men can even remember all the types of insurance they need today, never mind paying for them. Life insurance.

Health insurance. Major medical insurance. Car insurance. House insurance. Disability insurance. Liability insurance. Boat insurance. Business insurance. Often, there isn't enough money available to do all that should be done.

He feels money pressure from the *commitments* hanging over his head, the *shortfalls* now taking place, the *needs* that are going unmet, and the *debts* that need to be repaid.

Over the years Jim's company subtly urged him to put on the trappings of success. The right car to park in the lot, the right house to signal his success, the right vacations to talk about during breaks, the right clothes to impress the company's clients.

The problem is, of course, that these symbols of success cost money—more money than Jim had. So Jim began to borrow money to pay for the accessories of a rising star. Oh, he didn't jump in. At first he just wiggled his toes in the shallow end by borrowing for a car nicer than he could afford or really needed. Then came the maximum mortgage on top of the down payment money he borrowed from his parents. One day, many years later, Jim woke up in the deep end of the pool, tired of trying to keep everything afloat, feeling like he was about to drown.

Today? Jim is running scared. He works seven days a week. He doesn't feel like he can fit church into his life right now. Once upon a time he read his Bible most days. No more. The trappings have become a trap.

THE PROBLEM OF DEBT

*I*n December 1995 a record 18.8 percent of after-tax income went to repay consumer installment debt (add in auto leases and home equity loans and the ratio increases to an unprecedented 21.6 percent).[2]

In my opinion, one of the five biggest practical problems facing men today is debt pressure. No pressure gets a man down like debt pressure. The pressure to repay debt can feel like the powerful tentacles of a giant sea monster pulling you down into the suffocating pressure of the deep.

Debt is simply borrowing from *future* income to buy what we cannot afford today from *current* income. Some debt, like a manageable-sized home mortgage, may make good sense. Most debt, however, does not.

Like a silky-voiced siren, our culture seduces men into the bondage of debt.

Like a silky-voiced siren, our culture seduces men into the bondage of debt. We often end up buying things we don't need with money we don't have to impress people we don't like. As said in *Wall Street, The Movie,* "The problem with money is that it makes you do things you don't want to do."

Why do men go in debt? Because they are not content with what they have. Here is a great truth: If you are not content where you are, you will not be content where you want to go.

Why doesn't it occur to many otherwise intelligent men that it takes more energy to earn a living *and* service a debt than it takes to just earn a living? Few men understand the pressure of debt until they feel it's weight. By then it's too late.[3]

The problem with debt is that you have to pay it back. All in all, the interest payments linger long after the shine fades away.

WORK

Work pressure feels like the throbbing pain of a toe swollen plump and purple by a splinter buried so deep you can't see it.

The splintery thorns of work include bossy bosses, crummy customers, horrendous hours, paltry pay, and rough relationships. The deadlines are too short, the crises too tall, the projects too pressured, the quotas too high, the budgets too low, and the plans too aggressive to meet or beat.

One man put it this way, "My greatest pressure definitely comes from my work. Every moment is scheduled. I go from meeting to meeting to meeting. I am bombarded with decisions—big decisions—all day long. Frankly, I love it. But it's exhausting. I'm not taking care of my health any more. I really need to get back to exercising."

Another man said, "I feel a lot of pressure on my job. I'm not getting any younger, and I just have this sense the company would love to ease me out and ease a younger man in."

Yet another man said, "The pressure to perform is horrific. If I can't get the job done, there are a dozen other guys standing in line who think they can."

Christian men feel a special burden in their work. Even though work has been made difficult by the Fall, Christian men must work enthusiastically, as working for God. "Whatever you do, work at it with all your heart, as working for the Lord, not for men" (Colossians 3:23). Not a few men find this difficult, and many haven't heard of this principle at all.

Your husband may feel work pressure because he loves his work too much or doesn't like it enough (or at times, both).

Men Who Love Their Work

Work can be intoxicating. Made for the task, men deeply enjoy working on important projects, meeting deadlines, being brought in to give their opinions. Meeting ambitious goals or solving complex problems turn a man's crank like few things can. We'll talk more about this in the next chapter, "Work: Why Men Are Preoccupied with Work."

The more he loves his work, the more projects he takes on, and the greater the pressure. For many men their work becomes their mistress. An increase in work may lead to a decrease in romance. One man told me that he loved his work so much and worked so hard that he had lost much of his appetite for sexual intimacy. This is not an isolated case.

Men who hate their work

A second possibility is that your husband hates his work, or at least doesn't enjoy it. Research shows that as many as 80 percent of all people may be employed in jobs not suited to their aptitudes.[4] Yet, because of financial and family responsibilities, many men feel trapped. Feelings of frustration often come at the very moment he has fathered children and taken a big mortgage.

One reason some husbands don't enjoy their work relates to the different ways men are wired. Consultant Bobb Biehl has identified that every man (and woman) has a "burnout clock," which starts ticking at different points. Depending on how your husband is motivated, he will become bored with his work at different stages. See if you can recognize which of the following five types best identifies your husband. Think how knowing this can help you better accept him for who he is.

1. *Designers*. These men prefer the theoretical world to the practical. They love to create theoretical solutions to theoretical problems. Don't ask him to do the practical work of coming up with a working model. Examples could include business consultants, medical researchers, and academicians. Once he has solved the problem in theory you can hear the burnout clock start ticking. To continue in the project will lead to frustration and boredom.

2. *Designer-Developers*. These men prefer to not only define the problems, but come up with original solutions, and even develop a working prototype. Examples might include software designers or systems salesmen. But, near the end of the development process he hits the wall and rapidly loses interest.

3. *Developers.* Developers like to start with two or three working models or examples and then adapt what's best from each one to create a new, synthesized model that improves on the working models. Examples could include a teacher or a coach. Once that goal is reached "or two years and one day" (to quote Biehl) have gone by, you can hear the burnout clock ticking.

4. *Developer-Maintainers.* These men are fine-tuners and de-buggers. They would rather work with an existing system, organization, or project and solve the practical problems of making things run smoothly. Examples might include opening a branch office or trouble-shooting a plant that shows red ink. However, once things are running smoothly (Biehl suggests four or five years into the project) this man wants to take on a new challenge.

5. *Maintainers.* The maintainers like jobs in which the policies and procedures are clearly spelled out. They excel at keeping existing systems functioning smoothly. Examples could include property managers and power company maintenance personnel. This man doesn't change jobs much. His burnout clock might not tick for twenty or thirty years.[5]

Once a man's burnout clock starts ticking, it's time to find a new challenge. Hopefully, he can do that within the context of his existing job. The most frustrated men at work are often those who are burned out because God "designed" them one way, but they are working another. If your husband shows the telltale signs of burnout, why not have him read these few paragraphs.

PEOPLE

People pressure feels like a crown of thorns pressed by a "friend" into your husband's brow that punctures him with unexpected pain.

The late Tom Skinner, a sought-after speaker, once told me that he received a call one day from a friend who wanted him to speak at an event one week away. Usually such events get scheduled months in advance.

Tom looked at his calendar and said, "I'm sorry. I have an appointment with my daughter on that day."

The most frustrated men at work are often those who are burned out because God "designed" them one way, but they are working another.

"Oh," his friend came back. "Then you could be available on that day. We really need you, Tom. We're depending on you. Will you do it?"

"I don't think you understand," Tom replied. "I have an appointment with my daughter that day and I can't break it."

After two or three more attempts from different angles his friend gave up. What was particularly interesting is that they wanted Tom because the speaker they *really* wanted had to cancel at the last minute. So, his friend was all too prepared to sacrifice Tom's relationship with his daughter on the altar of his urgent need.

Few pressures your husband feels exceed the expectations placed upon him by friends and loved ones. Few pressures weigh more heavily on him than how to balance the competing priorities of his wife, his kids, his boss, his customers, his coworkers, his friends, and his pastor or priest.

One day I asked a man if he thought a mutual friend could help out on a project. "Ned's strung out," he replied. "He can't say no to anyone. He has way too many irons in the fire. He isn't very effective with anything he's doing. He'd say yes, but he really doesn't have the time to follow through."

Nothing would help this man more than for his wife to help shield him against overcommitment. He could say, "I'd really like to help you out. I'm real busy right now. Let me talk this over with my wife and get back to you." It's sort of like saying, "Well, I'll have to check with my boss." It takes the decision out of his immediate hands. That way, he doesn't have to feel that unpleasant pressure of not wanting to say, "No."

Once a television talk show host wanted me to appear on his show three nights in a row to raise money for his station. I was tied up on a deadline at the moment he called, so my secretary relayed the message. I told her I needed to pass. When she called him back he gave her no small amount of grief—he was offended I wouldn't do it and more offended that I didn't call him back myself. I can appreciate how he felt. On the other hand, I'm quite positive he's not going to be at my funeral. And even if he was, I know he wouldn't cry. But I do have a wife and two children who will. Why do I feel so much pressure to make people happy whom I don't even know that well? I don't know the answer, but I do feel the pressure.

The best way for a man to manage his people pressure is to decide in advance how much time he wants to set aside for his relationships with God, his wife, and his children. Then, whatever is left over can be devoted to vocation, ministry, recreation, and lending that helping hand. One idea that works well for one man is to eat breakfast and dinner with his family every day, and to never work on weekends.

RELIGION

Religious pressure is like walking barefoot through a sandy lot filled with sand spurs. Once you're in the middle of the patch, you still have to walk back over those fishhooked spurs to get out!

The church can put a lot of guilt-inducing pressure on a man. A man gets the feeling, "If you truly love God you'll be in church on Wednesday night."

Actually, one man has a great policy. When he started attending his church he told the pastor, "Look, I can give three hours a week to the church. I can give them to you any way you want, but that's all I've got available to give. If you want me for three one-hour services on Sunday morning, Sunday night, and Wednesday night, fine. If you want me to teach Sunday school, fine. But then I can't come Wednesday nights. If you want me on a missions committee, okay. But with all my other priorities I still can only give you a maximum of three hours a week."

A lot of ministry today pulls men out of the home to tell them that they need to spend more time at home.

At first his pastor was a little offended. Later, on reflection, he saw that all of his men should probably think through a similar commitment. He realized he could ask men to think strategically about how much time they should give to the church, and how.

It would be funny if it wasn't so sad. A lot of ministry today pulls men out of the home to tell them that they need to spend more time at home.

HOW YOU CAN HELP YOUR HUSBAND

Time Pressure. In the ebb and flow of life every husband will have periods when the cumulative demands from family, work, and church swamp his boat. During these seasons it's important for your husband to feel he has your unconditional support. On the other hand, what starts out as a temporary time can often turn into habit. Help your husband see when a season of time pressure has become a pattern. Perhaps you could ask your husband, "What are your three or four top priorities in life?" And, "Does the way you are investing your time really reflect those priorities?"

Money Pressure. Jointly decide on a lifestyle level. Don't push your husband into a pressure zone. Encourage him to take time out for self-examination and discover his own personal comfort zone. Follow the lead of corporate America and "right size" your home. (For another angle on this, read the subheading "The Myth of Super Dad" in chapter 12.) If you are not already on a budget, consider together establishing one.

Work Pressure. First, let your husband rest. Jesus didn't say, "Come unto me all you who are weary and burdened and *I will give you more work to do.*" Obviously, there are household chores for your husband to do. Strike a good balance. Talk it over. Second, help your husband rest. Don't "dump" the day's problems on him when you first see him at the end of the workday. Find out from him how much time he needs to unwind before tackling the home front. Perhaps he works it out on the road before he gets home. Maybe, like me, he likes to wash up, change into jeans, read the mail, and relax for fifteen minutes. You both need realistic expectations. Talk it over and see if you can agree on a "procedure" that works for both of you.

People Pressure. We all need to feel needed. Your husband may come in contact with many or few people during the day. Whatever the case, be the person he most wants to be with. Men are to love their wives, and wives are to respect their husbands and support them. You may or may not be receiving the love you need. Give him the respect and support he needs. You can win him by your own unwavering behavior (see 1 Peter 3:1–3). Then, as he continues to surrender more and more to God he will love you more and more.

Religious Pressure. Do not use religious language to prove points or make your case during arguments. If your husband tends to work too much in the church, suggest that he decide in advance how much time he should devote to the church in view of all his priorities.

A THOUGHT FOR HUSBANDS

What do you throw overboard first when you come under pressure? For most of us it's our quiet time, our wives, and our kids. Why is it that we tend to give so much of our time to those who care about us so little, and so little of our time to those people who care about us so much?

In this chapter we discussed some of the pressures husbands feel from time, money, debt, work, people, and religion.

Sometimes it can be difficult for our wives to understand the pressure we feel. Other times, however, they understand all too well but we have our own plans, and we are not willing to "hear" our wives.

You may be frustrated with the amount of pressure you're under. Enlist your wife to help you manage your pressures. Is she part of the problem? If so, you need to talk about that. Would she be willing to listen to you if you would open up more? Probably.

Why not elevate the moment, take your wife to dinner, and tell her in advance that you want to share with her all the sources of pressure you feel under right now and learn about her pressures. Perhaps both of you can make a list in advance so you'll remember everything you want to say. Listen to each other without criticizing, giving advice, or giving an overly quick reply. When you both have everything on the table, discuss ways to reduce the pressures you both are feeling.

If after some time to sort things through you find you are still under too much pressure you may need a spiritual medic. Get with a friend or counselor and go over everything that's causing pressure and frustration in your life. Make some decisions. Ask that person to hold you accountable by asking you once a week how you are doing.

Five ❧

Work

Why Men Are Preoccupied with Work

When their third child arrived, Jim and Sandy decided that Sandy, a college graduate with a good career, would give up her job to stay home with the kids. This decision put the full financial responsibility on Jim's shoulders.

A few years later, Jim's pastor approached him about serving on the elder board of their church. Partly because of their earlier decision for Sandy to work in the home, Jim, an architect, already spent a lot of time at the office. In fact, to keep up with his workload he worked many nights until 9:00.

Jim felt honored to be invited to serve but, as he and Sandy talked it over, they realized there already were not enough hours in the day. In fact, Jim not only declined to serve as an elder, he also made an appointment to see his boss.

"Sandy and I have been thinking," Jim began. "I would like permission to begin leaving the office early enough so that I can have supper with my family every day." After some further discussion, his boss agreed. Not long after, however, Jim was passed over to become a partner in the firm.

Jim reflected on what has happened, "We made two major decisions. First, that my wife wouldn't work outside the home and, second, that I would be home for dinner every day. The net result was that I have been passed over to become a partner in my firm. But that's okay. I'm happy in my work now."

Many people will immediately think, "What a shame! No bigger house and no partner!" But the Bible does say, "A man's life does not consist in the abundance of his possessions" (Luke 12:15). Jim and Sandy both know they have chosen the better way.

What's most remarkable about this story is how infrequently we hear about others doing the same.

What role does work play in your husband's life?

A MAN'S DESIGN

As a clock must tell time, as a camera must take pictures, as an apple must fall to the ground, as the sun must rise, as the stars must twinkle, so must a man work. A woman may work outside the home, but a man has no biological choice. A woman's arms are made to cradle children; a man's arms are made to swing an ax.

Work tends to be a man's most comfortable activity.

Work tends to be a man's most comfortable activity. One man put it this way: "I am propelled by an innate drive to bring home the venison." Another man said with some shame, "The easiest thing I do is go to work. The hardest thing I do is come home."

If a man is not happy on his job, he is not happy. A wife will tend to direct her creativity toward her children. A husband wants to direct his creativity toward his work.

Men are designed, or "bent," to be occupied with their work. God created men with a strong back, two good hands, a brain, and a desire to achieve and conquer. Work is commanded (2 Thessalonians 3:10–12; Genesis 1:28; 1 Timothy 5:8). Work is commended (Proverbs 24:33–34). Hard work is a biblical value (Colossians 3:23; Ecclesiastes 11:6). A man has to work—it is a rule of life. God "hard-wired" husbands to work.

THE IMPORTANCE OF YOUR HUSBAND'S WORK

A man began teaching high school math after college. He said, "After a few years I have identified two problems I think God is calling me to deal with. First, my students are coming to class with problems that math can't solve. Second, the Christian teachers at my school don't know each other." He is praying for a vision about how to respond to these two needs. He said, "I am an ordained math teacher."

Every man has been "ordained" in his work. (Women, too, whether inside or outside the home, but that's a different book.)

If you looked up the word "secular" in a Bible concordance, how many references do you think you would find? The correct answer is "zero." That's because God makes no distinction between *sacred* and *secular*. The notion that we perform secular jobs *or* go into the ministry is a cultural idea not a biblical one.

It's not just that our work is something we do to give us a platform to do ministry, it is ministry.

The first time my FedEx man stepped out of his van to deliver my package I knew two things: First, he loved God (I was pretty sure, and he confirmed it); second, he understood that his job *is* his ministry. *It's not just that our work is something we do to give us a platform to do ministry, it is ministry.*

Every vocation is holy to the Lord. Our vocation, or work, is an extension of our personal relationship with God. Ninety-five percent of us will never be in "occupational" ministry, but that doesn't mean we are not ministers. So, the issue isn't whether or not your husband is in ministry, but whether or not he is *faithful* in the ministry to which God has "ordained" him.

There is intrinsic value in your husband's work because it makes life more livable, creates jobs, contributes to an orderly society, creates income to meet family obligations, satisfies his need to be significant, and fulfills the biblical mandate to "fill, rule, and subdue" God's creation.

Work is a priority for a man. At the same time, a man must strike a balance with his other priorities.

WHEN OCCUPATION BECOMES PREOCCUPATION

Occupy means "to engage or busy oneself." Preoccupied means "to be excessively concerned or distracted." How and why do husbands move from occupation to preoccupation with their work?

As men, we tend to become preoccupied with our work because we find it exhilarating, because that's where our self-worth is tied up, because of pressure from our employer, and/or because it's the only way to keep up our lifestyle. Let's look at each of these temptations more closely.

ADDICTION

Men become preoccupied with their work through addiction. They become addicted because their work gives them strokes. It's scintillating. And it's the thing they *can* do well.

The addicted husband has a strong work ethic. He would rather work than eat and often does. His significance tends to be rooted in the feedback he gets at work. He loves the pressure, the scent of a big deal, the camaraderie.

The workaholic honestly thinks he works this hard for his family. That's because in the beginning he did.

Many times the problem is a habit. As one man said, "I enjoy doing whatever is in front of me at the moment." He enjoys his wife and family just as much, but sometimes he gets "excessively concerned" about his work and gets "distracted."

Many men know they are worka-
holics but still do nothing about it. Near
the end of his career a friend's wife
stepped off a curb, was struck by a
passing van, and died. He said, "I
always thought, I'm going to build my

The workaholic honestly thinks he works this hard for his family.

organization. I'm going to work hard. Then we'll have time together. Now that will never be. Now I realize that life is paper thin."

IDENTITY

A friend took early retirement from the organization he founded and for twenty years served as its chief executive officer. About three months later he received a check for about $3,000 to settle some outstanding matters from his old employer.

He pulled up to the drive-in teller window of his bank and told the clerk he wanted to deposit $2,000 and he wanted the rest in cash. The clerk was nice but explained that she couldn't give him the cash at the teller window.

"You don't understand," he told her indignantly. "I can tell you everything you need to know to prove I'm the same person to whom that check is made out."

She said, "I'm sorry, sir. But there's nothing I can do. That's just the bank policy."

"Let me talk to your supervisor," he said, beginning to gather a head of steam.

"Yes, sir. May I help you?"

"You certainly can," he began, then explained again what he was trying to do.

"I'm afraid she's right, sir. We're not allowed to disburse that much cash at the teller window."

"Excuse me, but this is my money and my account. I can give you every detail you need to prove I'm who I say I am. I can give you the exact date the account was opened, my exact balance, and the precise date and amount of my last deposit," he said confidently.

"I'm sorry, sir. I just can't give you the cash, but if you'd like to pull over and come inside the bank I'll be happy to take care of this for you."

At that he said, "Just forget it!" He jerked his car into gear and roared away fuming. When he arrived home he related the story sheepishly to his wife and said, "In ninety days I've gone from who's who to who's that."

Later he learned he would not have been able to withdraw cash at the teller window even if he had still been a chief executive officer. This, of course, only made him feel more silly.

How common for men to have too much of their identity wrapped up in work. It seems the more successful the man, the more closely he links how he's doing to how his career is going.

Men become preoccupied with their work when that's where their self-worth is tied up. Here's the problem: If *what* your husband does is *who* he is, then who is he when he doesn't do what he did anymore? This is an excruciating problem for men and, to secure their identity, they often become preoccupied with their work.

In the movie *Courage Under Fire*, Denzel Washington played a career army officer of seventeen years. During a crisis of faith in the army, he left his wife and family for a brief time.

Later, sitting in a car in front of their home, as they tried to patch things up his wife tried to console him and said, "I've learned how to be an army wife. To give it up would be no sacrifice."

"But it's my life!" he retorted.

"So are we," she said.

SURVIVAL

On a number of occasions I have heard that a woman's greatest fear is that something will happen to one of her children. Men, of course, fear this too. A man's most conscious fear, however, is that he will not be able to provide for his family.

Many men become preoccupied with their work because of pressure from their employer or a fear of losing their jobs if they can't keep up with expectations.

A man's most conscious fear is that he will not be able to provide for his family.

Al said, "I was in sales all my life. I'm grateful I always had a job, but no matter how much I sold the company always wanted ten percent more. I worked my fingers to the bone and, when I retired, all I had was bony fingers."

Jim worked for a major electronics company. "I loved my job, but I was required to carry a portable phone at all times." He said, "I felt like I was on an electronic leash. What starts out as a good tool becomes a crutch. Instead of people looking in their own files for information that would be readily available, they just call on a whim. It adds a lot of pressure."

The man trying to survive fears the downsizing business climate. One executive at a major chemical company reports that ten years ago the average work week for his company was thirty-eight to forty-two hours. Today it's forty-five to fifty hours. A man may not have much choice, except to take another job or demote himself.

LIFESTYLE

Sometimes men become preoccupied with their work because it's the only way to maintain the family's standard of living. We live in the generation that doesn't eat leftovers.

A husband with four young children learned that his sales management position was being restructured in a way that would cut his annual income by about $10,000. To qualify for the $180,000 home they had only recently purchased, his wife was already working part-time.

He became depressed and withdrew from his family. Their marriage had already been at the breaking point anyway. He asked her to go back to work full-time. Why? To keep the house.

When a husband must work excessively to support a lifestyle, the family is living "at" or "above" their means. Life may (or may not) appear serene, but below the surface the husband feels immense pressure to keep this overloaded boat from sinking. They possess many new and beautiful things, but the husband constantly feels a pressure to perform.

The problem with a big lifestyle is that the man becomes like a locomotive engine. He has to be at the next stop every thirty days to pay bills no matter what. When the family keeps adding cars to the train he has to expend more and more energy to cover the same ground. He feels the pressure to keep piling on wood or he knows it will stall out in the middle of the tracks.

Financial expert and radio broadcaster Larry Burkett has said, "If you are not living on the man's income you are living beyond your means." It's a philosophy, not the Bible's, but it's worth chewing on.

If you have a mini-warehouse, you probably have more stuff than you really need. "Better one handful with tranquillity than two handfuls with toil and chasing after the wind" (Ecclesiastes 4:6).

HOW YOU CAN HELP YOUR HUSBAND

A man's work is his calling. If your husband is not happy on his job, he is not happy. He is designed, or "bent," to be occupied with his work. Work is commanded and commended. Every man has been "ordained" in his work.

Working long hours from time to time is normal, necessary, and even a healthy part of life. There are times a man just has to do it.

You can encourage your husband to hold a high view of his vocation. Every vocation is holy to the Lord. Sending him off to an honest day's work brings him fulfillment and enables him to provide for his family—his deepest concern.

Work is a priority for a man. At the same time, a man must strike a balance with his other priorities. As men, we tend to become preoccupied with our work because

- we find it intoxicating—Addiction
- that's where our self-worth is tied up—Identity
- of pressure from our employer—Survival
- it's the only way to keep up our standard of living—Lifestyle

I do think that working long hours from time to time is normal, necessary, and even a healthy part of life. There are times a man just has to do it. For example, when King David's troops went off to war they had to be preoccupied with the task at hand.

The problem comes when temporary projects become permanent hours. At some point a man must answer the question, "Where is your faith?" Psalm 127:2 says, "In vain you rise up early and stay up late, toiling for food to eat—for he grants sleep to those he loves." Wives, support your husband on his short-term projects and encourage him to trust in God when something needs to give. Encourage him to regularly evaluate his priorities.

Finally, are you putting undue pressure on your husband to make a lot of money?

A THOUGHT FOR HUSBANDS

We are created to work. For most of us men, work is our most comfortable environment. When a man is happy in his work, he is happy.

Work is a priority for a man. At the same time, a man must strike a balance with his other priorities. As men, we tend to become preoccupied with our work because

    ___ we find it intoxicating—Addiction
    ___ that's where our self-worth is tied up—Identity
    ___ of pressure from our employer—Survival
    ___ it's the only way to keep up our standard of living—Lifestyle

Rate how much you personally identify with each of these four statements. Mark a "1" if you strongly identify, a "2" if you somewhat identify, and a "3" if you don't identify with each statement.

Complete this sentence: I would characterize the amount of time I spend at work as

    ___ Underwork   ___ Balanced
    ___ Overwork   ___ Workaholic

Here are some questions to help you think more about how you are balancing your priorities.

THE "ARE YOU WORKING TOO MUCH?" QUIZ

- Do you consider yourself a workaholic?
- How many hours a week do you work?
- How long have you been working those hours?
- Are you "overscheduled"?
- Do you have a hobby?
- How do you unwind?
- How would your wife rate your marriage?
- Are you exercising?
- Can you rest?
- How much time off have you taken in the last three years?
- If you could do anything what would that be?
- How is your walk with God?
- Are you using your gifts?
- Is your burnout clock ticking?
- Are you having fun or just trying to get through it?
- Could you take a personal retreat?
- Would your wife agree or disagree with your answers to these questions?

If you did poorly on this quiz maybe it's time to reevaluate.

Six ❧

Temptation
The Six Persistent Temptations
Men Struggle With

*H*usbands respond to temptation differently than their wives. Women tend to flee temptation. Men like to slowly crawl away and hope temptation will overtake them!

WHY MEN STRUGGLE

*N*o man sets out to fail on purpose. Yet, every day we learn of men, godly men, who do fail. Why is that? Man has an adversary, an opponent. Seducing your husband to fall in love with the world is the opium of the devil. To entice your husband to become engrossed in the things of this world is to defeat him morally.

As the flame attracts the moth, so the world seduces men: "Come closer." Unless we men remain perpetually vigilant, we begin to do what is permissible but not beneficial (1 Corinthians 6:12). When a man lives too close to the flame, his own evil desires carry him away into temptation and sin. The devil would love to toast your husband.

We're helping you to see what your husband is like, what he's feeling inside, what he's thinking, and what he's going through. Remarkably, all men go through virtually the same set of temptations. The Bible establishes this, and experience bears it out: "No temptation has seized you except what is common to man" (1 Corinthians 10:13).

In other chapters we have covered or will cover struggles your husband faces with work, communication, fathering, spirituality, and being a difficult husband. In this chapter let's explore six particularly persistent temptations husbands face.

EMOTIONAL NEGLECT

Every morning she walks three blocks to the post office to pick up the mail. For the last three years a cheerful but comfortable young man has worked the counter.

They began to exchange pleasantries when she came for the mail and, in due time, they quite naturally started greeting each other on a first-name basis.

She was married to a good man but, as an ambitious young executive, his work consumed most of his time and all of his energy. Even on those evenings when he was home he always seemed preoccupied. During the first few years of their marriage she brought up her loneliness from time to time. But, with a wave of his hand, he would dismiss her concern.

She loved him very much, but the longing for intimate, meaningful conversation built up a pressure inside. One day the thought occurred to her: *He's never going to change.* For days she brooded as she mulled this thought over in her mind.

A few days later, when she went to pick up the mail, her postal friend noticed she looked a little down. "You look a little down today. What's the matter?" he asked.

"Oh, nothing," she answered firmly. He decided to leave it alone.

The next day she again appeared with long face and he decided to press her, "Come on, something's the matter. You can tell me."

"Oh, it's nothing really," she replied unconvincingly.

He kept his thoughts to himself, but day by day she became more melancholy. A week passed, and he couldn't hold back any longer. "You seem so blue," he said. "What's the matter, anyway?"

"Well ...," she hesitated. "It's not that big of a deal. It's just that my husband works so hard ... "

The postal worker, too, was lonely, and they began to commiserate over the counter. One day he took his break when she came in, and they sat at a picnic table on the side of the post office where they shared each other's pain. She began timing her walks to the post office around his break times.

She only wanted someone to talk to. He only wanted to be a friend. Neither one of them planned for anything to happen, but a strong emotional bond developed. One thing just led to another.

Your husband is most tempted to not give you the one thing you most need: emotional connection and intimacy.

While each of the persistent temptations we will explore in this chapter touch your life, nothing touches your life so personally as your husband's temptation to emotionally neglect you.

Your husband is most tempted to not give you the one thing you most need: emotional connection and intimacy. In our men's seminars the first thing we say about marriage is that a wife's greatest need is for intimacy. Intimacy means that I know who you are at the deepest level, and I accept you.

We tell men, "A wife wants her husband to give her the first place in his life in the same way she gives him the first place in hers." Even though men have heard this, sometimes for years, often it just doesn't connect. Wives naturally give their husbands first place. Husbands don't. As one attorney said, "My wife has told me for twenty-three years that she'd rather have half the money and twice as much of me."

Women are natu-rally drawn to an intimate love rela-tionship. For men it must be learned.

I believe the propensity for men to neglect their wives is at the heart of why God gave the command, "Husbands, love your wives, just as Christ loved the church" (Ephesians 5:25). It's worth noting the Bible gives no similar instruction to wives. Why is that? Wives are naturally drawn to an intimate love relationship. For men it must be learned.

Here's a letter I received that shows what happens when temptation gives way to the sin of emotional neglect.

> I am the wife of a very quiet man. He's so nonverbal that I take it as a personal rejection. I love people and am very outgoing.
>
> Sometimes I feel like we must fight just so I can get him to notice me or talk to me. We have been struggling for a long time with this. I love him, and we are both Christians. I try to be a good wife, and a good mother. I suffer from low self-worth because he doesn't build me up. I feel that he has a critical spirit toward me and only finds fault with me.
>
> If you could stress to men that women have a great need to be told kind things like, "You are pretty ... That was a good meal ... I'm so glad that you are mine," it would really do wonders for their marriages. I feel starved for these kind words.
>
> I try to treat him the way I want to be treated. I tell him he is smart, a good dad, a good husband. I know this doesn't come naturally for him to be verbal or very encouraging. But I think if you could help those quiet-

by-nature husbands who are married to outgoing wives you'd be helping lots of marriages that struggle with communication.

All I need is a little kindness, especially verbal. I need him to be my best friend. I'm tired of "makeup" sex. I need love. As it is we have had an emotional divorce.

LUST

Mike loves God with all his heart. Yet, he made a regular practice of checking out beautiful women. One day he realized what he was doing was sinful against his wife. He made a commitment to stop looking and lusting.

"One day not much later," Mike said, "I was sitting in a restaurant just finishing my meal. Out of the corner of my eye I noticed a very sensual woman walk into the restaurant. I was determined that I was not going to look at her and lust.

"I didn't know what to do, so I prayed and asked God for help. As it happened, there were about three peas left on my plate. I decided to focus on those peas and began to stare real hard.

"I felt like my head was caught in a giant tug-of-war. One force pulled my jaw upward to look at this woman. The other force yanked my eyes back toward those three peas. It was a bare-knuckles brawl between old habit and new commitment. My face was half twisted toward her, but my eyes bulged out to stay glued on those peas.

"Finally, the battle began to subside. A few moments later it was over. I had won. God gave a spiritual victory. I still am tempted to lust, but God has given me the power to have victory every time I ask his help."

One day a few months later, Mike took his wife to lunch. As they waited for the check she said, "Mike, I've noticed you don't look at women anymore. I just wanted to tell you that I appreciate that. Thank you very much."

Any man who says that he doesn't struggle with sexual temptation is either lying or he isn't heterosexual.

Away from home for a conference, seven pastors went to lunch together and were waited on by a strikingly beautiful, sensuous waitress. The chemical reaction was palpable. The sexual temptation they felt was so arresting that each man muttered his order into his menu so as not to stare. As she went to the kitchen to place their orders they all sat speechless staring at their place mats. You could hear the sexual energy crackle in the air.

Any man who says that he doesn't struggle with sexual temptation is either lying or he isn't heterosexual.

Finally, the senior man broke the ice in his own inimitable way. "Well, God made the heavens and the earth."

They all nodded agreement. "Oh, yes."

Then he said, "All that is and all that is in them he made."

"Yes, that's right," they agreed.

"And he made humanity," he continued.

"Yes, God made humanity," they chimed in perfect cadence.

Then the senior pastor glanced toward the kitchen door where their waitress had disappeared, nodded his head and said, "He made some nifty humanity, didn't he?"

They all howled, and the spell was broken. Nobody said a word, but as they looked around the table they could see it in each other's eyes. *I felt it when she walked up to the table, did you feel it? Yeah, I felt it. I forgive you, do you forgive me? Yes, I forgive you, are you all right? Yeah, I'm all right.* And it was over. But it happened. It happened because that's what happens to men.

Men become sexually stimulated visually. As one man put it, "My three greatest temptations are money, pride, and bikinis." The visage of a shapely woman walking down the street or a scantily clad model happened upon while flipping through a magazine bursts into a man's mind like a guest who doesn't knock.

Perhaps the most important thing for you to know is that when your husband does look and lust, it in no way means he doesn't love you. Yet, it is a temptation that must be managed.

I saw the mailman in our driveway recently. I never get the mail. It's been years since I've gotten the mail. But, since my wife wasn't home, I thought I would try to do something nice and help out. As I walked back in the house and thumbed through the mail, an unsolicited Victoria's Secret catalog leaped at me, teeth bared, trying to attach itself to my jugular vein. I threw it down and got out of there!

Focus on the Family magazine, January 1993, disclosed that a remarkable 37 percent of pastors confess inappropriate sexual behavior with someone in the church. What does that suggest for the men in the flock?

The velocity of today's culture leaves many men drained of the spiritual energy needed to reflect on their temptations and the moral energy to resist them.

In an earlier life Eddie was one of the boys. He was never "evil" but, like many young men, Eddie was prone to talk about women and stare at the wrong kinds of pictures. Eddie married and soon after yielded his life to a personal faith in God. After his first child was born Eddie began to seriously settle down.

At his Bible study one morning the group discussed sexual temptation. After the meeting Eddie, a Christian for less than two years, pulled the leader aside.

"I need to talk about this," he said. "Frankly, I'm somewhat relieved. I thought I was the only Christian man alive who struggles with lust at the level I do. I've got it bad. Some days the temptation is such a spiritual battle all day long that I am completely exhausted by the time I get home."

The velocity of today's culture leaves many men drained of the spiritual energy needed to reflect on their temptations and the moral energy to resist them.

A highly respected man was taking a walk in the predawn hour. As he passed by one home he noticed the light was on behind the translucent glass of a large bathroom window.

Because no creature was stirring, and because pitch black engulfed the rest of the street, he was startled to see the outline of a woman who seemed to be dancing or doing exercises behind the window.

"I've been walking with the Lord for a long time," he said. "I had just finished a beautiful quiet time with the Lord. Yet, in the blinking of an eye, some force lunged toward me and tried to drag me toward the window for a closer look. I got out of there as fast as I could, but it frightens me that it could happen at all."

We live in a sexually overstimulated culture. A new sexual ethic puts every man closer to the edge of sexual temptation. There's really nowhere to turn. What thirty years ago would have been reserved for "girlie" magazines now appears every day in underwear ads of the daily paper. A man would have to wear a blindfold to escape this temptation.

Sexual temptation, of course, is nothing new. Even Job, the friend of God, acknowledged the temptation to lust: "I have made a covenant with my eyes; Why then should I look upon a young woman" (Job 31:1 NKJV).

The best way to resist sexual temptation is to flee. After becoming married, a man insisted on keeping up his habit of visiting questionable massage parlors. His interest was not therapeutic. Frantic, his wife called her husband's best friend to intercede, and the friend attempted to reason with him. Today that man lives a completely pagan lifestyle, and has abandoned his wife and children.

FALSE GODS

When Bob Buford turned forty-four he surveyed his vast accomplishments and was struck by a case of "success panic." *Is this all there is? How much is enough? Now what?*

What makes Bob's story particularly poignant is that he was not a backslidden, lukewarm Christian. Anything but that. He taught Sunday school, had a great marriage, no harmful habits, and no skeletons in his closet.

He decided to hire a leading strategic planning consultant to help him with his private life. "In my hour of deepest need, grace led me to an atheist," recalls Bob.

As they began their session Bob raised his issues. *What should I do? How can I be most useful? What are the values that give purpose to my life? Who am I? Where am I going? How do I get there?*

After the consultant listened he asked just one question. He said, "What's in the box?"

Bob was caught off guard. "What do you mean? Please explain."

"Well, I've been listening to you for about two hours and I can't put together an honest plan for you until you identify the mainspring. So, I'm asking you what's in the box? For you, it is either money or Jesus Christ. If you can tell me which it is, I can tell you the strategic planning implications of that choice. If you can't tell me, you are going to oscillate between those two values and be confused."

After contemplating the implications for a few minutes he said, "Well, if it has to be one or the other, I'll put Jesus Christ in the box."[1]

Incidentally, despite all his fears of having to become a missionary or go to seminary, God left him in virtually the same roles—but with a whole new perspective.

Bob's story is every man's story. Not many Christian men are tempted to worship an idol *or* God. Rather, the temptation is to worship an idol *and* God. Many men try to put two (or more) things in the box.

Most men conceal some secret ambition that competes with a full surrender to the lordship of Christ.

Idolatry is the error of giving worship or homage to any power or object other than God.[2] When a man seeks the God he wants—the one who will spoil him and let him have his own way—he makes an idol. Cultural Christians are not worshipping the God who is, they worship some "other god," an idol.

Whether they crave accomplishments, money, pleasure, possessions, power, prestige, or position, men are, as John Calvin said, "idol factories." That's our job. We manufacture idols. Most men conceal some secret ambition that competes with a full surrender to the lordship of Christ. They try to put two things in the box.

MONEY AND DEBT

The chief idol among men is money and the things money can buy. Men find money intoxicating. Often, the church rewards men for loving money.

An old country preacher put it this way, "If a man gets drunk on whiskey we put him out of the church. If a man gets drunk on mammon we make him a deacon."

Materialism is the "ism" a man can love. In *The Man in the Mirror* I told the story about how I manipulated my wife so I could end up wearing a solid-gold Swiss watch. Here's the rest of the story. Later, God convicted me of my motives. I felt so guilty I sold the ostentatious watch. But then I turned right around and bought a second watch just as expensive, but not obviously so. It's an addiction that's hard to give up. (Eventually, I sold the second watch too.)

Jesus named money as his chief competitor. He put it this way in the Bible: "No one can serve two masters. Either he will hate the one and love the other, or he will be devoted to the one and despise the other. You cannot serve both God and Money" (Matthew 6:24).

The temptation is not to love God *or* money. The temptation is to love them *both*. The temptation for men is to try to have their cake and eat it, too. It's to add Jesus to their lives but not give up their secret ambition. Unfortunately, a man cannot love both. So if he clings to money he will eventually despise God.

Perhaps the greater problem today is not that men are tempted to *earn* more money, but that they are tempted to *borrow* more money than they can really afford to repay.

A debt-free pastor wrote to me and said,

> Over seventy percent of my men are in farming and ranching. If I say something to them about my view of debt, their response is, "Yeah, but you were never in farming. You can't make it in this business without large loans and taking on debt."
>
> Three of my men are entering a home construction venture. "Looks real promising," they say. But it involves big loans from the bank.
>
> Some of my men are under almost unbelievable stress. Hail, drought, and harsh weather have made this year especially disappointing.
>
> One of my best men was advised by his lawyer a year ago to declare bankruptcy, which he didn't do. "I'm

looking to lose $50,000 this year," he told me last Sunday. He is really under pressure and stress—and is working his tail off! Scarce is time for his precious wife and two teenaged children.

What is your counsel to these kinds of Christian men? Can one "make it" in business, construction, farming, or ranching today without all this risk, pressure, and large debt?

What advice would *you* give this pastor?

The Bible doesn't encourage debt. In fact, the Bible is full of cautions against debt and offers much counsel about how to overcome the negative consequences of becoming ensnared by debt. Further, debt is *never* recommended.

When any issue we face has no specific command in the Bible, our duty is to be wise. Here are just a handful of passages that offer us wise counsel:

- "The rich rule over the poor, and the borrower is servant to the lender" (Proverbs 22:7).
- "He who puts up security for another will surely suffer, but whoever refuses to strike hands in pledge is safe" (Proverbs 11:15).
- "A man lacking in judgment strikes hands in pledge and puts up security for his neighbor" (Proverbs 17:18).
- "Let no debt remain outstanding, except the continuing debt to love one another" (Romans 13:8).
- "Do not be a man who strikes hands in pledge or puts up security for debts; if you lack the means to pay, your very bed will be snatched from under you" (Proverbs 22:26–27).

Personally, I winked at these last verses, Proverbs 22:26–27, which caused me to go off the deep end. As a friend says, "We can choose our way, but not the result."

When the Tax Reform Act of 1986 was passed, all capital stopped flowing into leveraged real estate. I found myself with a mountain of personally guaranteed mortgage notes, no permanent financing in sight, a dried up equity market, an over-built marketplace, and no way out. I had ignored the wisdom of Proverbs and made a real snarl of my business life. It had taken me seven years to get into debt. Little did I know then that it would also take seven agonizing years to get out.

In January 1987 I was reading along in Proverbs and saw the following verses in a way they had never struck me before—they got personal!

> My son, if you have put up security for your neighbor, if you have struck hands in pledge for another, if you have been trapped by what you said, ensnared by the words of your mouth, then do this, my son, to free yourself, since you have fallen into your neighbor's hands: Go and humble yourself; press your plea with your neighbor! Allow no sleep to your eyes, no slumber to your eyelids. Free yourself, like a gazelle from the hand of the hunter, like a bird from the snare of the fowler (Proverbs 6:1–5).

Until the Tax Reform Act of 1986 my overarching business goal had been "to develop 10,000,000 square feet of commercial space by August 28, 1992." From the moment these verses connected with me "existentially" I made the overarching goal of my life "to get completely out of debt." I applied the Proverbs 6 principle. Though it took seven painful years to accomplish, I can say that today I owe no man anything except the continuing debt of love.

To be debt-free has released enormous creativity and energy. No longer am I consumed with plotting and scraping to make debt payments. No longer am I unable to get back to sleep when I awaken at 2:00 A.M. No longer am I a slave to lenders. No longer do I feel like some sea monster is dragging me under—I have caught my breath. No longer do I feel the stress in my marriage. Indeed, it takes less energy to earn a living than to earn a living and service a debt.[3]

If your husband (or you) are struggling with the pain of too much debt, ask yourself, "Is it worth all the stress and strain?" Perhaps together you can make a plan to alleviate some of the pressure by selling some debt-laden possessions. Perhaps a tighter budget would help. Pray for wisdom. Even if it takes as long to get out of debt as it took to get in, the years which follow will be a joy.

WHINING

Do you have a man in your life who is a whiner?

The Bible reveals a long history of whiners. Throughout the Bible people grumbled about the sufficiency of God's care—the pursuing Egyptians, the manna that wasn't good enough, the giants that made them look like grasshoppers.

One of the most persistent temptations husbands face is to grumble. Why are men so tempted to whine? The basic issue is whether or not your husband has accepted his lot in life. If he hasn't, and especially if he doesn't feel things are going his way, he will be tempted to grumble and whine.

When your husband sees other men advancing more rapidly, frequently resentments, jealousies, envy, and bitternesses build up. Slights, perceived and real, grind on his ego.

To understand why men are tempted to whine, two points are worth noting. First, we don't live in a garden anymore. We've been locked out (Genesis 3:23–24). The world is no picnic. Instead, it's a briar patch, a rock garden, a concrete jungle. Scott Peck begins *The Road Less Traveled* with the words, "Life is difficult."[4]

Second, there are thorns and thistles in life, and God put them there for our benefit and because he loves us. Thorns and thistles are the way we grow. A baby eagle won't leave the nest until its mother removes the feathered bed. Not until those sharp branches poke the little eaglet does it get motivated to grow to the next level.

Men tend to think, *If I could just get back into the garden, everything would be all right.* But one can't unscramble an egg, as they say. You can't rewrite history.

When babies throw a tantrum, they whine and cry until they realize they can't get what they want. Once your husband accepts his lot in life—that he doesn't live in a garden anymore, that those nest branches are poking him for his own good—he will stop feeling tempted to whine, and get on with the positive program. As the apostle Paul said, "I have learned to be content whatever the circumstances" (Philippians 4:11). For Christian men who are whiners, it's time to get over it.

When a man becomes a Christian he is by nature either a positive or negative person. Unfortunately, the tendency is not to change. But the decision to become a Christian carries with it a responsibility to become a positive person, and an obligation not to be a whiner.

Believers work the same ground as nonbelievers. A man's task is to help the world see a difference between how believers and nonbelievers respond to the briars, thorns, and thistles.

PRIDE

*I*n the early 1840s a young doctor, Ignaz Semmelweis, was promoted to oversee a maternity ward. He noticed that the women who became sick and died were the ones examined by teachers and students.

He instituted a policy on his ward that every physician and medical student who participated in autopsies of the dead must carefully wash his hands before then examining living maternity patients.

Until he established his new rule, fifty-seven women had died. After instituting the washing rule the mortality rate plummeted, strongly indicating the fatal infections were carried from the dead to the living.

Later a group of doctors, after following Semmelweis's procedure, entered the maternity ward and examined a row of twelve patients. Eleven of those women developed temperatures and died.

It dawned on Semmelweis that not only was the fatal disease carried from the dead to living, but also from the *living* to living. Thereafter, all doctors were ordered to wash carefully after examining *each* patient. Howls of protest went up about all the washing, but the mortality rate went down even further.

But, instead of celebrating Semmelweis, his peers belittled him so much that his annual contract wasn't renewed. His successor threw out the wash basins and mortality shot back up, but they still refused to believe.

Eight months later Semmelweis finally landed another similar position in Budapest. He reintroduced the same washing procedures with the same results but, astonishingly, his colleagues refused to even speak to him.

He documented his findings in a book which was met with bitter sarcasm. The strain was so great that his mind finally snapped, and Ignaz Semmelweis died in a mental institution.[5]

Today our understanding of germ transmission is taken for granted. Yet, for many years the "pride of man" kept this knowledge from becoming common preventative practice, even in the face of overwhelming evidence. How deeply man's pride can darken his mind.

In 1973 a relatively minor burglary of an office in the boomerang-shaped Watergate building facing the Potomac River in Washington, D. C., toppled the presidency of Richard Nixon.

Yet, it was not so much the burglary, nor even the cover-up, that galled people so much. Rather, it was Richard Nixon's stubborn pride. Instead of pretending he did nothing wrong, what if Nixon had appeared on television at the very first, admitted his error, and apologized? People can be very forgiving.

The same thing happens in our marriages. Stubborn pride often keeps the husband (or wife) from humbling himself and admitting he's wrong. Men can be hard-headed. Pride causes some men to feel they are "above" talking about "touchy feelings," and so emotionally neglect their wives.

Temptation to pride comes in more packages than you'll find in Santa's sack.

Temptation to pride comes in more packages than you'll find in Santa's sack. The most common form is for a man to look down with disdain on others, like the proud Pharisee who was glad he was not like the tax collector who beat his breast and called out for mercy. Pride is a sin of comparison in which a man compares his (perceived) strengths with another's weaknesses.

Just as insidious, however, is the temptation for a man to look up in disgust on others who have it better or have accomplished more.

Once my company built a suburban office building with a parking garage. We moved our corporate offices there, and I was assigned a space in the special executive parking section of the garage, the section most convenient to the building.

We assigned these special parking spaces to the executive staff of tenant companies, while the rest of the workers had to scramble for the first-come-first-serve spaces.

So that I would have the full sensitivity of what it was like to park in the "general" section of the garage, I decided to spend a few days "competing" for the unassigned spaces available to everyone.

Each day I would park and walk by executives getting out of their cars. I thought I sensed a subtle, snobby, better-than-thou attitude. It was probably an overactive imagination on my part, but it really ticked me off.

I began to develop an intense pride that I was not so uppity that I had to park in the "snob section." I became proud of how humble I was.

Within a week I had a real problem. I had only intended to park in the "general" spaces for a few days to get the feel of things. But as I became aware of an acute case of "reverse pride," I realized I needed to work through my emotions. I couldn't move to the executive parking area until I stopped feeling so much superior to the executives because of my "humility."

Incredibly, it took nine long months to work through my pride and get to a place that I didn't resent those executives when I walked by. Finally, the Lord released me, but not until he showed me how easily I am tempted to the pride of life.

Pride is often a young's man disease. A young man often believes he can accomplish whatever he sets his mind to. He thinks he knows more than everyone else. He has a feeling of self-sufficiency.

Like most men, I felt like I knew more than my parents in my teens, more than my wife in my twenties, and more than my business associates in my thirties. God's grace helps a man move from pride to humility by seasoning him with the hard knocks of time. From the forties on, most men start to mellow out.

HOW YOU CAN HELP YOUR HUSBAND

You know your husband. You know his persistent temptations. Review the list:

- Emotional Neglect
- Lust

- False Gods
- Money and Debt
- Whining
- Pride

Perhaps your husband knows his problem, or maybe he's unaware. Whether he's aware of it or not, he most certainly finds his temptations embarrassing. Your greatest contribution will be to help him; your greatest challenge, not to embarrass him. Perhaps you could suggest he read this entire chapter, then you can discuss it together. Ask him, "Which of these are temptations that you struggle with on a regular basis? How do I contribute to your being tempted? How can I pray for you?"

As a wife, your greatest contribution will be to help your husband; your greatest challenge, not to embarrass him.

I realize how deeply you can be affected, even devastated, when your husband succumbs to these temptations. It can shake up the security of your world. Because you love him you will stand by him, but let me encourage you to look to Christ for true security.

A THOUGHT FOR HUSBANDS

Oscar Wilde once said, "I can resist anything except temptation." A former pastor who fell into sexual sin, said, "Christian men bang on Satan's door so they can flirt with temptation." Why do we act so surprised when he answers?

In this chapter I have explained to your wife six areas in which we men are persistently tempted ....

- Emotional Neglect
- Lust

- False Gods
- Money and Debt
- Whining
- Pride

Take some time to review the main ideas under each sub-heading, then answer the following questions:

1. Which of these temptations are persistent in your life?
2. Describe in one sentence the price you have paid in your relationship with your wife for yielding to temptation in each area you have struggled with.
3. Resolve to study the Scriptures for each area of persistent temptation. Accept the authority of the Scriptures, surrender your life in faith, and walk in the power of the Holy Spirit.

Part Two

Seven ⁊

Companionship
What a Husband Needs
from His Wife

Recently my wife, Patsy, and I attended a surprise appreciation dinner our friend Ben hosted for his wife, Julie. We had never heard of such a thing, and agreed to attend with no small amount of curiosity.

All the guests arrived at the banquet room a half hour before Julie. Ben gathered us together and told us Julie thought she was coming to a church fellowship dinner. Apparently, no one had spilled the beans!

When Julie arrived we all showered her with mushy greetings, and she started to become suspicious. Ben, however, still wasn't ready to let her in on our little secret. For the next thirty minutes Ben stonewalled as Julie repeatedly probed him for information.

Finally, the guests were seated and Ben said, "I would like to thank each of you for coming this evening. Julie, these friends have gathered here tonight to support the children and me as we express our appreciation to you for being such a wonderful wife and mother."

Ben went on to admit that he had made many mistakes. He confessed that often he was preoccupied with his work. He thanked her for hanging in there with him. He expressed gratitude for the great job she had done with the children.

After dinner Ben introduced a male vocalist who sang several love songs dedicated to Julie. Then a chaplain offered a stirring devotion. Each of the children shared a story about "mom" and gave her a gift. Ben concluded the evening with his own tribute and then presented Julie with flowers and a plaque which says, "1996 Wife of the Year Award."

You are the only real friend your husband has.

You've never seen a more stunned person in your life. Trust me.

It was a glorious evening. What struck me most was that I had never before been to such an event, and doubt I'll be invited to another any time soon. Only one in a million husbands will ever do anything quite like this (I know the idea would never occur to this dull writer). Yet, most men do love their wives deeply, even if they have trouble expressing it.

A HUSBAND'S GREATEST NEED

*M*ay I tell you something that you may at first find hard to accept? You are the only real friend your husband has.

However deeply he shares with you, or not, you are the one with whom he shares most deeply. By degrees, most men are loners. As a man told his wife, "I don't have any *real* friends besides you."

A survey I conducted while researching for this book asked men to complete a number of open-ended sentences. One sentence read, "My greatest need in marriage is _____." As you might imagine, men gave a wide range of answers. As the answers were analyzed, however, the two major themes which emerged were *companionship* and *support*.

A MASTER PLAN

God created light. God saw that the light was *good*.

God created sky, land, and seas. God saw that these, too, were *good*.

God created plants and trees. And he saw that the plants and trees were *good*.

God created the moon, sun, and stars. God saw that they were *good*.

God created the birds and fish. God saw that they, also, were *good*.

God created all kinds of animals. God saw that the animals were *good*.

God created man. And God saw that man was *good*.

Then God feasted his eyes on all that he had created and it was not only good, it was *very* good.

Then God strung his heavenly hammock and took a rest.

Soon God put the man in a garden and said, "Work and take care of this place." So the next morning when the sun came up, the garden grew, the rivers flowed, and the man punched in and went to work.

God noticed two problems. First, everything he had made was not only *good* but *very* good, except that the man was alone, and, well ... that was *not* good. The first problem God recognized was that it was not good for man to be alone.

Need #1: The Problem of Being Alone—Companionship

As a young soldier in the army, I remember the ache of being alone. Buddy talk can only go so far. I had no one to make plans with, no one to share a dream with. After the military I attended the university, but found myself alone all over again. Every man reaches a point at which he craves someone with whom to share his life. I was in that place.

One day I saw Patsy walking down the street and thought, *Now there goes the woman I would like to spend the rest of my life with.* I asked her, "Would you like to go out Friday night?" She said no, but that's another story. Finally, though, after several tries she did agree to a dinner date.

After we dropped off the couple who had joined us for dinner, we went back to my college studio apartment. My neighbors had gone away for the weekend and I was under orders to feed their fish, so she helped me. We talked. We laughed. We explored each other's lifeviews, values, and dreams. We played music and talked about favorite songs. We talked about what animated each of us.

Before we knew it, the sun peeked through the window. We had literally stayed up all night talking! We couldn't get enough of each other. I knew that this was the woman I wanted to give myself to, the one I wanted to serve and make happy. Later I learned that Patsy, too, had felt the same way.

More than anything else your husband needs and wants a life-long partner and companion.

It should come as no surprise to you that your husband's greatest need in marriage is *companionship*. Men express this need with words like "love, affection, a commonality, connecting, time alone together, happiness, growing love, closeness, someone to share life with, complete intimacy, physical affection, touch, a lifelong partner, a best friend."

More than anything else your husband needs and wants a lifelong partner and companion. He hungers to share with you the dreams, the sorrows, the joys. What husbands are saying is, "I like me best when I'm with you."

It was a terrific career, but it required Curtis to travel every week. Since he was gone two, sometimes three, nights a week his wife and children made the adjustment. They built busy lives of their own.

When Curtis did arrive home he sensed that neither his kids nor his wife had really missed him that much or, for that matter, cared that he was now home. When he would suggest they do something together, everyone already had their own plans.

Curtis began to struggle with feelings of hurt and rejection. He felt his wife didn't appreciate the sacrifices he was making to provide for his family. He took the rebuffs (real or perceived, who knows?) personally. During repeated attempts to talk it over with his wife, she dismissed his feelings as being too sensitive and assured him, "I love you very much."

Your husband will never know lasting joy and fulfillment until he learns to faithfully love and serve you.

Secretly, though, he felt she didn't need him anymore, and that the children satisfied all of her needs for love. The feelings of rejection and isolation intensified over the years. After numerous unanswered pleas for attention, one day he moved out.

Husbands, expressive or not, have a God-given need for companionship that can only be met by their wives. When wives don't meet this basic need for love and affection (often we tend to think of this as only the wife's need and forget the husband needs this too), their husbands become discouraged.

Not only does your husband have a built-in need for you to give yourself to him, he has a built-in need to give himself to you. Your husband will never know lasting joy and fulfillment until he learns to faithfully love and serve you. More than a few husbands have not yet grasped this reality.

If the first problem God noticed was that it is not good for man to be alone, what's the second problem?

Need #2: The Problem of Needing Help—Support

God "formed" man with specific purposes in mind, as a potter molds a vessel into the shape he wants. He stamped man with an identity, a replica of his own image. He commissioned the man to rule, fill, increase, and subdue the land. God hired the man as a landscape maintenance worker, wrote his job description, and told him to guard, protect, and attend to God's garden.

The second problem God recognized about man is that he needed help to accomplish these lofty goals. The task was too big and too lonely for the man to go it alone.

Here's what God did (humorous version). God said, "Okay, I can see that it's not good for this man to be alone. Now how can I solve this problem? I know! I'll give Adam a pet dog and name him Rover. He will be man's best friend.... No, that won't work. He needs a friend but he also needs a helper.

"I know what I'll do! I'll give him a workhorse. No?... Maybe an ox?... No, that won't work either. True, he needs a friend and a helper, but he needs someone to talk to. Hmmm....

"I know! I'll make another 'man' and they can watch football together, talk about cars, and play golf.... No, that won't work. He does need a friend and a helper and someone to talk to, but he also needs someone to help him subdue the earth....

"I know! I'll start a company and give him coworkers to help him care for the garden!... No, no, that won't work. The garden is not the only place where the man needs help. He needs help at home, and he needs help to fill the earth with others like him. This man, look at him! He needs help everywhere!

"Let's see. He needs a friend so he won't be alone. He needs a helper to do his work. He needs a companion to talk to. He needs help at work and at home. And he needs a helper to make little men. Hmmm....

"I know! I've got it! I'll make a woman!"

So, God did two things: He made a woman and he instituted marriage.

Marriage is a mysterious, spiritual fusion of two distinct lives into one flesh. What was the man before woman was taken from his body? Alone and needing help. The creation of woman and marriage was always anticipated by our omniscient Creator.

Marriage is a mysterious, spiritual fusion of two distinct lives into one flesh.

It will also come as no surprise to you that your husband's other great need in marriage besides companionship is for *support*. Men express this need with words such as "more understanding, support, encouragement, trust, safe haven, appreciation, respect, affirmation, acceptance, feel important." What husbands are saying is, "Help me out here," and "I need some encouragement."

In a national survey conducted for Promise Keepers, men were asked why they kept their promises. The two answers given most often were *participation in church-based small groups* and *supportive wives*.[1]

A dear man sent this insightful letter:

> I have to admit that I am among the group that did not return your survey about what husbands wish their wives knew about men for your book. Sorry! Please allow me to share what I feel is vitally important for women to know about men.
>
> Wives, we are not nearly as emotionally strong as we put on. Yes, we are decision makers, but we often struggle

with even simple decisions. Yes, we are great hunters, warriors, and competitors, but we desperately need strong encouragement and support from our wives.

God has blessed me with a beautiful bride of thirteen years who knows how important that encouragement is to me. Recently I had to leave town on a business trip for one week. My wife hid a note in my luggage, knowing I would find it at the end of the day when I unpacked in my lonely motel room.

It reads, "I love you, honey! Thank you for being such a special husband. Someone who cares about his family enough to get up at early hours and go to work to support them. A man who spends much of his time and energy with his son and his friends, teaching them. A man who spends time with the Lord each day to lead us in Christ.

"How wonderful that the Lord led me to you! I pray for you daily, my love. I thank him for you, that he gave you to me to spend my life with. I pray that he will give you strength and peace and joy. I hope this week goes quickly for all of us. I pray God keeps you safe. I love you more now, honey, than the day I said till death do us part."

I don't share this out of pride but thankfulness. I am a traveling man and motel rooms can often seem more like prisons. I have struggled for several years with thoughts that God is leading me to do something else, something where I would not be away from my family so much. Can you see how comforting and good a note like that from your wife can make you feel! It remains in my Bible and I read it whenever I need that encouragement boost.

A small thing? Perhaps, but not to the man who keeps this note in his Bible. Why would a man do that?

MARRIAGE IS A DIVISION OF LABOR

*F*or 60.7 percent of married women, helping their husbands means working outside the home.[2] Financial help is certainly support. For others, it means managing their homes while their husbands win the bread.

Whether your "support" is financial, emotional, and/or domestic, what your husband wants and needs most is the sense that you're both in this thing together. That he is appreciated. That as the (usually) primary breadwinner you will support him on the home front. That we can divide the labor and conquer.

On my son's soccer team every player has an assigned position on the field. Through practice each player becomes excellent at what he does best. By practicing as a team, they learn how to work together efficiently. Then, during games, even an observer can sense a chemistry and a harmony. As each individual plays his own position as part of a larger team, they are able to pass the ball skillfully around the field until one man is open to score.

The best marriages have an "agreed upon" division of labor. They don't just "let it happen."

A well-thought-out division of labor is a beautiful thing to watch, whether it's an athletic team, a business, a family, or a marriage—especially if everybody appreciates the contributions of the others. The best marriages have an "agreed upon" division of labor. They don't just "let it happen."

CAUSE OF DEATH: A BROKEN HEART

*H*is name was Lee Burke. Together with his wife, Mae, he eked out a small living running a restaurant at the old train depot in Albert Lea, Minnesota, and worked a small family farm in nearby Hayward.

It was about 1928. One of Mae's six sisters, Ida, had married well—to Mr. Erickson, the banker in Albert Lea. Lee Burke must have done something awful, because his brother-in-law, Mr. Erickson, told him, "Get out of town." And that's just what he did. Lee Burke abandoned his wife and four children. Harry, the oldest, was ten. Turns out Lee Burke was a con man, a flim-flam artist, a bad apple.

Not long after he abandoned Mae, she had a stroke. From that day on she slurred her words and dragged one leg behind her. Soon they lost the farm and moved into town to live with two of Mae's other sisters, Rena, a widow who owned a house, and Nina, who had never married.

To help support the family, young Harry went to work on a bread truck before school, at the butcher shop after school, and at the filling station on weekends. Later his baby brother, Bob, helped out on the bread truck and delivered papers to make money. They would rouse out of bed at 3:00 A.M. and had a permanent tardy slip for school.

Nina really did the hard work of raising the kids. She earned a small wage operating the elevator in the local bank building. On the way home she would stop at the grocer's, who gave her free run to buy whatever she needed and pay whatever she could. If she owed $50 but could only pay $20, well, that was fine. People pulled together.

One day Mae was listening to a radio program from Fargo, North Dakota, and heard her husband's name mentioned. He had been arrested for something; nobody remembers what it was for sure. That was the last they ever heard of him.

Lee Burke was the alias that Harry Sidney Morley used after he abandoned his family. Lee Burke was my grandfather.

Grandma died when I was a toddler. Some say she died of a broken heart. My mom says Grandma often held me in her arms, but I don't remember her.

The subject of my grandfather has always been touchy, but recently I was able to ask my father about him. He said, "I never missed him. I didn't mention him because of mom."

In 1961 Lee Burke contacted my father and his other three children. After thirty-three years, only my Uncle Harry showed any interest. He travelled with his wife and three children to Peoria, Illinois, to meet him. He was living in government-assisted housing, a broken old man.

When Patsy married me she married my history, too—a history she knew virtually nothing about. Part of who I am today is a rejection of who my grandfather was. We have all heard stories about men repeating the sins of their fathers. My dad didn't. I really appreciate that my dad chose to break with the past. Thanks, Dad.

When I married Patsy I, too, married her history. I thank God that both my father and Patsy's father set a clear example of how I am to love and cherish my wife.

I think there may be a little "Lee Burke" in all men. It's the panicky feeling that comes over a man when the walls start closing in. We have probably all thought about chucking the whole thing, men and women alike, at some point.

Most husbands, thank God, would never seriously consider abandoning their families. They will fulfill their divine responsibilities. However, when wives befriend, encourage, help, respect, and support their husbands they take a huge step toward inoculating their marriages against death by broken heart.

CONCLUSION

It is true that more men are developing strong male friendships through accountability groups, but even then there remains a certain guardedness. As Oswald Chambers said, "What is the sign of a friend? That he tells you secret sorrows?

No, that he tells you secret joys. Many will confide to you their secret sorrows, but the last mark of intimacy is to confide secret joys."[3]

Rejoice when your husband acts like that little boy. You are the only one for whom he will act so silly. You are the best friend your husband has ever had.

HOW YOU CAN HELP YOUR HUSBAND

As a youth an African American friend of mine perfected a "don't mess with me" strut to let the other boys know he was tough. Sometimes when he would walk through the front door at home he would forget what mode he was in. His mother would say, "Okay, you can cut that out right now! You're home, mister!"

As men we work hard to send vibes that we are self-sufficient, have everything under control, and that "we're cool." But you know better. "We're home now."

Life beats us up (husbands and wives alike). There's a war going on out there, and we come to home base to have our wounds nursed. We come home because, though we love doing what we're called to do, we need relief from the battle. Let's be companions. Let's figure out how to mutually support each other through a division of labor. These are, after all, the two problems God wanted to solve by making two of us instead of one.

What is the area in which you have given you husband the greatest support? Think of an example of how you have been a companion and friend to him.

How do you think your husband would rate you on the following scales?

"My wife is my closest companion ..."

Always   Usually   Sometimes   Rarely

"My wife supports me ... "

Fully   Most of the time   Somewhat   Not at all

Based on your answers, is there anything you need to do?

A THOUGHT FOR HUSBANDS

*T*wo of the greatest needs we men have in marriage are *companionship* and *support*.

The best way to get what we need is to practice the foundational rule of civilized societies everywhere: "Do unto others as you would have them do unto you."

When we invest into the emotional well-being of our wives with time, conversation, meaningful touch, unconditional love, acceptance, encouragement, humor, and friendship we release them to fulfill their destiny as a friend and helper.

When we invest into the emotional well-being of our wives, we release them to fulfill their destiny as a friend and helper.

What is the area in which your wife has given you the greatest support? Think of an example of how she has been a companion and friend to you.

Sometimes we tend to take our wives for granted when our needs are being met. Rate your wife on the two following scales:

"My wife is my closest companion ... "

Always   Usually   Sometimes   Rarely

"My wife supports me ... "

Fully   Most of the time   Somewhat   Not at all

Why not let her know how much you appreciate her companionship, friendship, encouragement, and support? Ask her if she agrees with your answers. Have a brief discussion about how you can be better friends.

We are wired not only to *need from* our wives, but to *give to* our wives. We have a built-in need to give ourselves to the woman in our lives. To be truly happy we must faithfully love and serve our wives. Have you been doing this? If yes, congratulations. If no, what should you do?

Eight ✑

Physical Intimacy
What Else a Man Needs
from His Wife

*B*oth partners in a marriage desire and need physical intimacy, which includes both *sexual intimacy* and *nonsexual touching.*

Almost inevitably, though, each partner wants or needs more of one than the other. Usually, the husband wants more sex, while the wife wants more touching.

THE POWER OF TOUCH

*S*everal years ago the dreams of a young engaged couple shattered when a horrible highway accident left him in an irreversible coma at twenty-three years of age.

The husband wants more sex, while the wife wants more touching.

His fiancée said, "I had no reason at all to hope, until I noticed on one of the monitors that his heart beat faster when I talked to him."

The doctors dismissed this as coincidence, but she began visiting him every day. She would sit at his bedside talking to him, caressing him, and kissing him. Her mother said, "They spend hours together and it's been like that for four years. I've never managed to count how many kisses she gives him."

In early 1995, after four years in a coma, he regained consciousness.[1]

Touch releases power. It's like taking jumper cables and attaching a live battery to a dead battery.

Men, like women, respond to touch. Near the beginning of the AIDS crisis I remember watching a news broadcast of Princess Diana shaking hands with an AIDS patient. That single act of touching had a profound impact on my whole thinking, as I'm sure it did for others.

Touch is one of God's most powerful forces. A woman in the Bible thought, *If I can only touch the hem of Jesus' robe ...* When she actually touched his robe he stopped and said, "Who touched me? ... I know that power has gone out from me" (Luke 8:43–46).

In an experiment at the University of Miami Medical School's Touch Research Institute, researchers gave premature babies forty-five minute massages every day. Within the short span of ten days, the massaged babies showed a forty-seven percent greater weight gain than babies not regularly touched.[2]

Touch converts *potential* love into *actual* love. Touch releases power. It's like taking jumper cables and attaching a live battery to a dead battery. When we touch there is a transfer of energy from one person to the other.

I love to be touched by my wife, Patsy. In fact, I can't get enough of it. Your husband loves to be touched too. It's not just a "woman" thing.

THE GIFT OF SEXUAL INTIMACY

Sexual pleasure is a beautiful gift of God for married couples. Biblically speaking, sex is good! Sexual intimacy should bring the greatest bliss, joy, pleasure, oneness, and happiness of human life.

Yet, many couples spend a lifetime struggling in this area. At one of those perfunctory business cocktail parties we attended, Patsy overheard a man and two women talking about how often they made love with their spouses. After she recovered from swallowing her tongue, Patsy heard one woman say, "My husband wants sex all the time. We women are the ones who have to do all the work." One drink later she added, "And I hate it."

SEX IS AN ISSUE

On Friday mornings I teach a Bible study here in Orlando to 150 men. These men come from forty-four different churches representing thirteen different denominations. Their ages range from early twenties to early eighties. We have executives, salesmen, business owners, truck drivers, firemen, laborers, elected officials, pastors, full-time Christian workers, and retirees—you name it. The point is, this is a very diverse, representative group of men.

One morning I said, "I would like to take a poll about how important sex is to men. I'm going to give you three possible choices: Sex is *no* issue to you, a *medium* issue, or a *major* issue."

When I asked them to raise their hands, no man raised his hand that sex is "no issue" to him. A handful of men indicated a "medium issue." Over 95 percent of the men raised a swaying forest of hands to say that sex is "a major issue" to them.

HUSBANDS WANT MORE SEX

Early in my career I was a part-time instructor for a real estate licensing school. One day I was walking with another instructor about ten years my senior from our Tampa hotel rooms to the meeting facilities. He was married to a stunningly attractive wife. As we walked along he said, "Really, I'm very happily married. We have a great marriage in just about every way. But, to tell you the truth, we have a really dull sex life."

Knock me over with a feather! I was twenty-four and newly wed. I couldn't imagine how it could be true. In the years since I have found this to be the norm for men.

A man's sex drive is one of his strongest drives, especially when unmet.

Sex is the number one thing husbands would like more of.

A man's sex drive is one of his strongest drives, especially when unmet. Sex is the only thing that brought King David to disgrace. Most men find it difficult to exercise control over their sexual arousal. Husbands are more motivated by sex than their wives. Generally speaking, it is simply not as strong a drive for women.

Virtually all men experience attraction, arousal, and temptation *several* times a day. It may be a woman's perfume, a newspaper ad for ladies underwear, a picture on a billboard, the way a woman dresses, a brush against a woman's arm, or a woman walking through the office.

If I could synthesize what I think I hear men saying it is this: "I know I need to be more sensitive to your needs, and I hope you will help me understand how to do that. I also need for you to be more sensitive to my needs. What I would really like is a little more aggression a little more often."

A man wants and needs an active romantic life. A husband needs physical love in the same way a wife needs emotional love. A husband needs sexual gratification in the same way a wife needs routine acts of kindness.

HOW HE IS WIRED FOR SEX

*H*usbands and wives come to the marriage bed with entirely different concepts and expectations. It's like putting the north pole and the equator in the same room.

Your husband views sex the way he views everything else in life. It's a *project*. He's a man on a *mission*. For your husband sex is sudden, it's impulsive, it's intense, it's raw, it's fast, it's furious, it's over!

Recently, a strategic planning consultant introduced me to the business concept of the "critical event." The idea is, what must happen at the lowest level in an organization for the company to be successful? For example, for Coke it is that someone pick up a can of Coke rather than Pepsi. For Delta Airlines it's that someone buy a ticket. What do you think would be the critical event for arousing sexual desire in your husband?

A husband needs sexual gratification in the same way a wife needs routine acts of kindness.

Almost anything. For a man arousal is visual, instantaneous, and complete. He can be aroused when he accidentally sees you partially clad or wearing that favorite flannel pajama shirt, as he watches a romantic movie, if three days go by, or even while he reads this paragraph!

HOW SHE IS WIRED FOR SEX

*W*hat is the "critical event" for the wife? For wives sexual desire is a by-product of many small kindnesses done throughout the week. For her, desire bubbles up from deep wells of intimate conversation and sharing with her beloved husband. It is a response to the nonsexual touching he invests in her during the week.

For wives sexual desire is slow, meditative, earned. Arousal is a choice she makes based on a response to the emotional love she receives from him. She views sex the way she views everything else. It is a *relationship*.

So, he says, "Let's make love, and then we'll talk!"

She says, "No, no, no ... Let's spend time drinking deeply of each other, learning to really know each other, and then make love to celebrate."

The difference? She wants a soul mate; he wants a lover.

She wants a soul mate; he wants a lover. Any couple can have a much improved sex life by understanding the sexual differences between husbands and wives. Wives, do you periodically speak to your husband about each others' priorities in sex? What are your husbands' sexual wants and needs? Does he understand your needs and priorities? He wants to be a fun and faithful partner, and he hopes you do, too.

HOW YOU CAN HELP YOUR HUSBAND

Touch your husband several times a day by kissing him, hugging, squeezing, patting, holding hands, and sitting close enough on the sofa to touch. Men love to be touched. Trade back rubs often.

Encourage your husband about how much you enjoy being touched, and give him specific examples of how. Remind him from time to time—no one can remember everything.

How would you rate your sexual relationship with your husband?

___ not an issue   ___ medium issue   ___ major issue

How do you think your answer would compare to his?

One thing I do know for sure, sex is the number-one thing husbands would like more of in marriage.

If I could summarize in one sentence what I think I hear men saying it is this: As mentioned earlier, husbands say, "What I would really like is a little more aggression a little more often." Your husband has a larger sexual appetite than he's probably letting

Sex is the number-one thing husbands would like more of in marriage.

you know. It is a very strong drive in his life, and many frustrations are removed when you enjoy the marriage bed often.

Is sexual pleasure a beautiful gift of God in your marriage? If not, are you struggling? If so, how much of it is because you have not been sensitive to your husband's desire for a better sexual relationship?

In the same way, you have emotional love needs. Be frank about how to meet each other's sexual and emotional needs.

Reread the sections *Husbands Want More Sex* and *How He is Wired for Sex*. Did you know this? Does this confirm what you suspected? How can the points raised in this chapter help you have a more vital physical relationship?

A THOUGHT FOR HUSBANDS

We men have a sexual drive altogether different from our wives. We want sex right now, and then on to the next project.

Our wives, however, want to enjoy sexual intimacy as a by-product of a deeper love relationship built on the foundation of regular conversation, meaningful time together, and small kindnesses done throughout the week—like holding the door, clearing the dinner table, and mutual help.

Also, our wives love to be touched—quick hugs, long embraces, pats on the arms or shoulders, squeezing her knee or hand, putting your arm around her shoulder, walking through the mall holding hands, kisses, and sitting on the sofa close enough to touch when you watch TV.

A major problem develops when you make physical demands on your wife without making emotional investments in return.

Plan to invest emotional love into your wife. Here are a few suggestions:

1. Touch and kiss your wife every day.
2. Talk to her about her day, tell her about yours. Be intentional about it.
3. Set a time to talk with your wife about your sexual relationship. (The more awkward this seems to you the longer you have probably put off what should be done regularly.) Just do it.

Ask your wife, "What are two or three things I could do to make our sexual relationship more meaningful and pleasurable for you?" Listen deeply without giving an overly quick reply. Don't get your feelings hurt by taking things personally. Acknowledge what you think you hear her saying. Discuss what you don't understand. Affirm your intentions. Finally, offer two or three suggestions that would make your sexual relationship more meaningful and pleasurable to you, also.

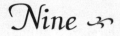

Nine ᴈ

Communication

What Men Want to Express But Find Difficult

*T*rue or False? Husbands are poor communicators. Before you answer, let's play with this for a while.

Our surveys show that wives have two great complaints about their husbands when it comes to communication. I asked my wife, Patsy, if she could guess what they were and the words rolled sardonically off her tongue: "They don't talk and they don't listen."

However, if you want to compliment a man about how he does his work what would you say? "Well, he gets things done." Okay, but why?

"Because he works hard." Okay, but how?

"Well, he's articulate. He knows how to get his point across. You can really understand him. He explains himself very well. Also, he's a good listener. He really understands the situation. You can really talk to him."

In other words, he can *talk* and he can *listen*.

So, are men good communicators? They can be.

Unfortunately though, he who is the "great communicator" at the office regularly comes home exhausted. Instead of "you can really understand him" and "he's a good listener" his wife must settle for impersonations of large zoo animals expressed in gruff, monosyllabic grunts.

Every living person, man or woman, is good at communicating about what's interesting to them.

His boss says he talks too much. His wife says he doesn't talk at all. Why is that? What's going on here? What happens to men on their commute between work and home?

Consider this: Every living person, man or woman, is good at communicating about what's interesting to them.

Men get a bad rap, but it's not because they can't communicate ... they do it all the time. It's simply that husbands like to talk about what they like to talk about. Not only that, wives like to talk about what they like to talk about too. Something has to give.

Women can talk to women, and men can talk to men. What's needed is for husbands to take a special interest in what animates their wives. Wives, of course, also need to make sure they're interested in the things that fascinate their husbands.

THE FIVE STAGES OF COMMUNICATION

*F*rankly, there's no reason—practically or biblically—for a husband to be a poor communicator.

There was a time when every husband couldn't get enough of his wife. What happened? We can discover the answer by observing how our communication as husband and wife goes through five stages.

Stage 1: Courtship

The courtship stage is a time of mutual fascination, curiosity, and attraction—in all ways. Couples enjoy long walks and longer talks, expressions of sensitivity come naturally, the warm glow of love abounds, and they cling to each other in syrupy displays of public affection.

They revel in each other's hopes and dreams. They resonate with each other's spirituality. It is a season of discovery: "How many kids do you want? What kind of work do you want to do? What are your—*our*—ambitions?"

The focus in courtship is on being together: "What we do we do together." Couples are trying to learn as much as possible about each other.

Her role in this stage is to prove she will love him better than any other woman he could ever find. His role is to prove he will love her better than any other man in the whole world. As one eligible bachelor said, "I want to give myself to a woman and serve her."

During the courtship stage the communication volume is full blast and around the clock. As I said in a previous chapter, when I finally convinced Patsy to go out with me, we literally talked nonstop until sunrise about a broad range of subjects. Everything I said was deeply interesting to her. Everything she said came to me as though from the lips of an angel.

Nothing can compete with communication in this stage. It's, "I can't get enough of you, babe." A deluge of conversation rages like a white water river. Our motivation to find out what's interesting to our potential mate is never higher.

The best way to describe communication during the courtship phase is to say that for him it is *a project* and for her it is *a lifestyle*. Women enjoy the *process* of communicating as much as the *results* of communicating. Men are typically not like that. Men want to get to the bottom line and move on.

Here's where we run into a bit of a problem.

When your husband was dating you he couldn't get enough of you. But, for him courtship was a *project*. It was the *task* at hand. Normally, what intrigues him are tasks, not relationships. He prefers to talk about facts, not feelings. He likes to discuss rational topics, not emotional ones. For him, communication is functional, to deliver information. Under normal circumstances he generally doesn't use words to help him clarify his emotions.

So he engages his future bride in a way that she interprets as the norm. In reality, he was only doing what it took to get the "deal" done. Once the deal was made, he was ready to move on to his next project.

During this phase, communication can be improved by asking the right questions and by learning the natural differences between men and women. Also, it's valuable to discover how you relate to the unique personality and temperament of the one with whom you would spend your life.

Stage 2: Honeymoon

The honeymoon stage is a time of anticipation, establishing routines, setting up house, getting to know each other in a new way, silly and selfish conflicts, pursuing dreams, establishing employment, and just generally having fun together.

The focus is on setting up the first apartment, negotiating the terms of a shared life, and working out kinks and quirks in the marriage knot.

His role during this stage is to establish a career and, also, to help his new wife set up the nest. Her role during this stage is to set up the nest and, also, to find work or a career if she will be among the sixty-one percent of married women working outside of the home.

During this stage the communication dial is set on maximum. They communicate morning, noon, and night. He calls her at work during the day. She packs notes in his briefcase or lunch bag.

At this stage, setting up "life" begins to compete with communication, but it's considered a nettlesome distraction from being together. Communication flows freely in a strong and steady stream full of exciting rapids. The motivation to discover what's interesting to our mate still runs high, yet hints of cooling down from the torrid pace of courtship begin to appear.

The best way to describe communication in the honeymoon stage is to say that for both of them it is *a pleasure.*

Improve communication during this stage by making a lifelong commitment to be "best friends." Underscore this commitment by studying the Bible and praying together, and possibly working through a couples' devotional book.

Stage 3: Building

The building stage is a hectic season of accumulation, expansion, and starting and raising a family. For the husband it is the time of his greatest strength, but also the season that consumes the greatest amount of his energy.

Suddenly, they find themselves out of time and out of money. The pressures cause many mistakes. The seriousness of the conflicts between them increases because the stakes are higher.

They focus on making ends meet and trying to balance priorities. It will be a long, twenty-five year run.

His roles during this stage include providing for his family, managing his career, and doing his work. Her roles include managing her home, managing her career, and doing her work. Together they work through the shared responsibilities of nurturing the children and taking care of the inside and outside of the house.

During this stage the volume of communication becomes, "Could you please turn that down? I'm trying to get some work done here." Communication takes place on a "need to know" basis. The husband operates as though he's under combat conditions: "There's a war going on out there!"

The competition for husband-wife communication at this stage is just about everything: work, church, children, car pools, early meetings, and working late.

The natural course, if untended, is to drift apart and become the proverbial two ships passing in the night. The motivation to find out what's interesting to your mate will never be lower. You and your husband fall in bed at the end of a long day exhausted by the demands. The problem with life is that it is so daily.

Communication can be improved vastly by carving out time to be alone together.

The best way to describe the building stage is to say that energy is *directed toward vocation* rather than communication.

While this phase is tough on marriage, communication can be improved vastly by carving out time to be alone together, learning to be frank about your needs and desires for time and conversation, being interested in what your mate is interested in, and planning in advance some questions to ask your spouse.

Stage 4: Empty Nest

Phewww! Are we glad to get beyond Stage 3 or what! The empty-nest stage is a time of gradually slowing down and finding some time on your hands. The question of the day is "What do we do with it?"

The empty nest is a time for reinventing your marriage and getting reconnected. It brings the realization of time wasted and of neglecting the person you really care about the most. For him it's a time of wanting to set things right and making sure she will be kept warm during winter.

Communication focuses on rebuilding an intimate, personal relationship that's deeper than diapers.

His role during this stage is to reduce his preoccupation with work and to refocus on her. Her role is to find new ways to invest time now that the kids are gone and to refocus on him.

During this stage the volume dial on communication is at first deafening silence, then the "soft, easy favorites" begin to play. You can talk all you want: "I never knew we would have this much time to ourselves." The only competition for conversation is baby-sitting the grandchildren.

Communication focuses on rebuilding an intimate, personal relationship that's deeper than diapers.

Communication has come full circle. It's about coming back home. You drink from still but deep waters. Your motivation is to find out what's interesting to your mate. You have a strong desire to learn how to reconnect.

The best way to describe communication in the empty nest stage is to call it *the key to happiness.*

Ways to improve communication include listening, asking questions, expressing love verbally, and commenting on each other's interests.

Stage 5: Widow- (or Widower-) hood

The final stage of marriage is spent sitting quietly beside an empty favorite chair. The light has gone out. It's dark inside. You sit alone. No one answers when you call out in the middle of the night. There's no one to talk to. It's all a memory now, whether bitter or sweet. There's so much to say, but it's too late.

Once, a long time ago, you were alone and lonely. Then you met. Now you have invested a lifetime together, into each other. Do now what you need to

Do now what you need to do.

do. Make sure that when one of you goes to God, though the other may live alone, they will not sit surrounded by the sorrows of what could have been.

WHY HUSBANDS WITHDRAW FROM CONVERSATION WITH THEIR WIVES

Once a couple hits full stride in the building stage of marriage the distractions, the familiarities, and the routines set in. Let's explore why husbands sometimes withdraw from meaningful conversation with their wives.

Differences

In the same way a just-snapped Polaroid picture becomes clearer with time, our natural differences become clearer the longer we're married.

Here are a few generalizations that can be useful if we don't try to push them too far. Her orientation is to relationship; his is to task. Her principal activity is nurturing; his is providing. Her principal concerns are family and security; his are money and meaning. She feels the need for intimacy—emotional connectedness; he desires to be significant—to make a difference.

Her conversations with friends focus on children, family, friends, people, and her nest; his "guy" talk revolves around football, tools, scores, golf, cars, business, and politics. Wives speak to give shape and form to what they are feeling inside; husbands speak to transfer information. When she asks the same question over and over again he doesn't get it. She wants to relieve the emotional tension building up in her heart; he thinks she's getting paranoid.

Make the effort to understand the natural differences between men and women. Learn to love your husband not so much in spite of how he's different from you but because he's different.

To Avoid Conflict

Love is blind during the cool evenings of romance, but sees 20/15 (a little better than 20/20) when the cloudless noonday sun begins to bake. Shortly into marriage couples discover they do have different goals, different expectations, and different values. The very differences that fascinated in the beginning create friction down the line.

Learn to love your husband not so much in spite of how he's different from you but because he's different.

Often a husband will come to believe he can no longer speak with frankness about important issues. A man went to visit a marriage counselor and immediately said, "I talk everything over with my wife." Then they proceeded to discuss a wide range of topics of vital interest to the man.

The counselor asked him, "What does your wife think of all that?"

"Oh," he blurted, "I would never mention these things to her. She wouldn't understand." In other words, "She wouldn't share my opinions and I want to avoid having arguments." Listen to the words of counselor Paul Tournier:

> Thus it is that in order to have peace many couples put aside certain subjects—those that are emotionally charged—those that are most important for their coming to a true mutual understanding. Thus, bit by bit, the transparent window which the relationship between man and wife should be becomes blurred. They are starting to become strangers to one another. They are losing the total oneness which is the divine law for marriage.
>
> When instituting marriage, God declared, "They shall no longer be two, but one." As soon as a couple begin to hide matters from one another they compromise

the basic oneness of marital life. They start off on the road to failure.... We may try to patch things up, start over again, attempt a reconciliation. But a real rebirth will always have as its condition a far deeper and more difficult mutual frankness.[1]

And so, to keep peace, husbands will often choose to leave well enough alone and go their separate ways. They will stick to talking about news, sports, and weather. Often they never go deeper than, "What's for dinner?" which is tantamount to withdrawing from the conversation.

If your husband doesn't communicate to you about his deepest interests or show an interest in yours, try to isolate how previous conflicts—and the way you have both handled them—may be part of the problem. Consider asking a counselor to help you both learn to express yourselves to each other with greater sensitivity.

To Avoid Criticism

Every human being fears criticism. That's because no one is satisfied with himself. Actually, men spend every waking hour living in such a way to avoid criticism. They try to meet the requirements of their jobs to avoid criticism. They wear clothes to fit in. They try to drive cars appropriate for their social class. Just like teenagers, men want to "fit in" with the culture of their peer group.[2]

Criticism of your husband is rejection by the one closest to him. When he hears, "Why can't you be a better father?" "Why can't you make more money?" "Why can't you get a better job?" something inside of him recoils. Eventually, he will pull his head back into his shell like a turtle.

One of the first things a counselor teaches the counselee is to express feelings, but don't critique the person. For example, if your husband said, "You're a terrible housekeeper," you will be offended. What you hear is an attack on the essence of who you are, not a critique of something you do. However, if your husband said, "When the house isn't clean it makes me feel irritable," he has expressed something about how he himself feels, but without attacking you personally.

In the same way, if you said, "Why can't you make more money?" he hears, "You're not successful enough; you're not a good provider." Better to say, "When we don't have enough money at the end of the month to pay all our bills I feel afraid and out of control." The first approach attacks his manhood. The second approach expresses considerately how you feel about the circumstances.

If you said, "Why can't you be a better father?" he hears, "You're not a good father." Better to say, "When you don't spend time with the children I feel like they are missing the joy of bonding with you."

The less threatening approach of expressing feelings will help keep your husband in the conversation.

To Avoid Unwanted Advice

Let's say your husband comes home from work and you ask him, "How was your day?"

During the day he encountered an extremely difficult threat to the major project he has been working on for weeks. Office politics are involved. He is beginning to doubt whether his boss fully supports him on this. Rumor is the project funding is in jeopardy. On top of that, he can't get the prototype to work the way engineering said it would.

He considers all this and answers you, "Fine." Then he retreats to the washroom.

Later in the evening, however, he wants to talk. When men are ready to talk, what they want is not advice but consolation. Men don't expect their wives to understand the nuances of their most difficult problems. What they do expect is a sounding board, someone to listen without offering an overly quick reply.

The whole concept of a "sounding board" is that boards don't talk. What a husband wants in his wife is someone who will listen. From time to time everyone has a problem they can't "sort out." The act of talking to a live person forces the mind to take those jumbled thoughts and organize them into clear, coherent sentences that will make sense to the person being addressed.

Men don't expect their wives to understand the nuances of their most difficult problems. What they do expect is a sounding board.

When his wife interrupts and offers advice that is personal, like "I can't believe he would stoop so low," this distracts him from sorting out the real solution he's looking for. Or, if she offers technical advice she has no training for, like "Why don't you get those engineers to rerun the test," he dismisses her advice. He thinks to himself, "She just doesn't understand what I'm going through."

Too many encounters like this and the husband will begin to withdraw from opening up to his wife about his work. After all, he didn't want advice, he wanted consolation and encouragement.

As his wife you can encourage conversation by saying, "Tell me more." If he is ready to talk, encourage it. It's your turn to listen. And then, let him know how meaningful it was to you for him to share what's going on.

I have two rules for advice:

First, it can be taken as a general rule that when your opinion is not asked for, neither is it wanted.

Second, there is no greater loss than the right advice given at the wrong time.

Tiredness At the End of the Day

At the end of a long day your husband is tired. Every husband has a "best" way for him to unwind before engaging the homefront "in basket." Some make the transition on the drive home. Personally, I have always enjoyed a fifteen-minute pit stop from the rat race to wash up, change out of my suit, and get a snack before pulling back onto the "home" track.

When a husband is repeatedly pressed into deeper conversations before he's ready to talk, he will withdraw.

You, of course, are tired too. You have your own ritual. Perhaps it's sitting on the porch for a few moments of quiet before beginning dinner. Maybe you recharge by talking over the school day with your children.

The problem is this: When you are ready to talk, is he ready to listen? And when he is ready to talk, are you ready to listen?

This is such a major problem for many couples. We must find a middle ground that works for both of us. It would be wonderful for you both to consider each other's recharging schedules and demonstrate sensitivity to each other.

A couple of suggestions: First, ask your husband what times of the day he feels comfortable and refreshed enough to listen to you about how your day went and family and work matters. Also, tell him when you most like to "talk things out." Take note of each other's preferences, seek the right compromise, then talk to him when he's ready to hear you.

Second, ask him what times of the day he most likes to unburden himself and talk about his day. Tell him the times of day when you are most receptive to "hear" him. Take note of each other's preferences, find the common ground, then listen to him when he needs, or wants, to talk.

A Lack of Common Interests

Let's say you attend a parent-teacher conference at your child's school. You enjoy a captivating conversation with her teacher because of the common interest. As you wrap up your visit the teacher turns the conversation to philosophy which you don't study, then to baseball which you don't enjoy. Suddenly, your interest in this conversation plummets. It's the same in marriage. When the conversation strays into unknown territory the interest just isn't the same.

Too often in marriage husbands and wives let each other stray too far from common interests. He likes to go to movies, you don't. You like to go out to eat, he doesn't. If they haven't made an effort to discover mutual interests, a couple can enter the empty-nest stage with nothing in common—a sure bet for troubles.

Your husband may like to take on home improvement projects, follow sports, debate politics, discuss current events, and share what's happening in his work. You, on the other hand, may prefer to review what's happened during your day, talk about what's going on in the children's lives, go over plans for Friday's dinner party, mention who you saw at your health club, and enjoy emotional bonding time with your husband. Without effort both spouses can withdraw into their own little worlds—worlds that don't have enough seating room for the other. Make sure to pursue a few common interests.

GOOD COMMUNICATION

Remember the question with which we began this chapter? "Husbands are poor communicators—true or false?"

Often, men are taught not to express themselves. Aristotle Onassis taught his son how to negotiate: "Your face is your sword." In other words, don't let your eyes, face, or tongue reveal your inner feelings. Executives learn to speak in the hushed tones of the boardroom. Too much animation is taken to mean a lack of self-control.

Most wives would report that their husbands are not good communicators—"They don't talk and they don't listen." At the same time, most men acknowledge that good communication is one of the greatest needs in their marriages. We can get together on this.

Husbands have much to learn, but they can learn to communicate. They do it all the time. Communication is a decision.

HOW YOU CAN HELP YOUR HUSBAND

What stage of marriage are you in? How would you rate your communication at this point? How does that match up to the description for your stage of marriage described in this chapter?

You can be a great encouragement to your husband and help him be a more effective communicator. Review the reasons husbands withdraw from conversation with their wives and consider ways you can help your husband love to talk to you the way he loves to talk at work.

1. *Differences*. Celebrate your differences. Love him in his weaknesses and not just his strengths. Help him understand how you are different.

2. *To Avoid Conflict*. Restore a complete frankness to your marriage without being argumentative. Conflict resolution should restore, not tear down.

3. *To Avoid Criticism*. Avoid making "you" statements; learn to express feelings. Focus on the problem, not the person.

4. *To Avoid Unwanted Advice*. Learn to listen deeply without giving an overly quick reply. Be a consoler, not a consultant.

5. *Tiredness at the End of the Day*. Learn your husband's rhythm. Know the best times and best places for conversation that gets beyond news, sports, and weather.

6. *A Lack of Common Interests.* Successful couples like to be together. They develop shared interests like bowling, reading, hiking, plays, going out to eat. Work at it, and find a few things you can enjoy doing together.

A THOUGHT FOR HUSBANDS

Wives have two great complaints about their husbands when it comes to communication: "They don't talk and they don't listen."

Is that really true? It depends. Think for a moment about how you might describe a man talented in his work. You might say, "He's articulate. I can understand what he's saying. He really knows how to make his point. He listens, too. He takes time to understand the situation. You can talk to him."

In other words, he can *talk* and he can *listen*. So, are men good communicators? They can be. Men often get a bad rap, but it's not because they can't communicate … they do it all the time.

To have good communication with our wives we need to take a special interest in what animates our wives. Our wives, of course, also need to make sure they're interested in what's important to us.

In the final analysis, good communication is a decision. Consider these reflection questions:

1. Are you a good communicator on your job? If yes, why? Are you a good communicator with your wife? If no, why? Moreover, if you are good on the job but not at home, why do you think that's the case?
2. "Men get a bad rap, but it's not because they can't communicate, they do it all the time. It's just that they like to talk about what they like to talk about. Every living person, man or woman, is good at communi-

cating about what's interesting to them." AGREE/DIS-AGREE. Why?

3. When we dated our wives we were interested in every little detail about their lives. That was our "project." How has understanding your wife and spending time with her in conversation slipped in priority for you? Is that right? What can you do about it?

4. Do you have the desire to have more meaningful conversation with your wife? If so, you must decide to do so—you have to make a decision. Good communication is a decision. If you feel comfortable with it, why not use the following suggested prayer, or one like it, as a way of committing to be a better communicator.

Lord, I confess that I have not given the time, attention, and priority to communicating with my wife that I should. By faith I now make a decision to turn things around, to make conversation with her a priority, to risk some things with her because I made promises and took vows that I would love her. This is how I love her—by giving her my time, by talking and listening to her. To recapture the romance of our marriage I pledge myself to lay down my life for my wife. I will make whatever adjustments are needed to be there for her, as she has been there for me. Empower me by your Spirit to keep my commitment. Amen.

Ten ✣

Resolving Conflict
Help Around the House
and Other Sore Spots

Our family purchased a new gas grill—the kind that uses those fake charcoal briquettes. Ninety percent of all grills sold today use the fakes.

After the first couple of BBQs, Patsy and I agreed the grill didn't produce that tantalizing charcoal-grilled flavor the brochure had promised. So one Saturday morning I went to the home improvement store to see what could be done.

I was surprised to learn I could pick from three choices of briquettes—lava rock, ceramic, and regular. After discussing the pluses and minuses of each type with a helpful employee, I "scientifically" made what I thought was the best choice.

The next evening we grilled hamburgers, but Patsy and the kids still didn't think the burgers tasted all that char-grilled. So I proceeded to explain to them all the "research" I had done and why this was the best option. Patsy didn't seem persuaded.

The following Friday and Saturday I traveled out of town to conduct one of our men's seminars, a joyful but energy-sapping experience. By the time I rolled in late Saturday afternoon, I was pleasantly surprised to see Patsy honoring my return by preparing a favorite dinner, which included BBQ chicken. She asked me if I would grill the chicken and added, "Oh, by the way. I had John (our son) put in a different type of briquette that I bought for the grill."

Now, I must confess a mild case of "Are you deaf? Didn't you hear what I said?" However, why upset the ambiance? So, I put on the chicken, set the kitchen timer, and started reading the newspaper.

Ten minutes later, out of the corner of my eye, I saw a small bonfire raging in the backyard. An oily cloud of smoke rolled across the yard. Through the glass on our grill I could see flames engulfing our chickens!

I leaped to my feet, raced to get a spray bottle of water, and vaulted over the lawn furniture. I jerked the lid open, started squirting furiously with one hand, while turning down the burners with the other.

Every drop of grease that splashed on a briquette was instantly bursting into flames. Finally, I was able to bring the roaring inferno under control.

When I turned over those pathetic little chickens, the crispy bottom sides looked like the smoldering remains of an animal sacrifice.

I thought, *Didn't I tell her I had done all the research? But, noooo! She wouldn't believe me. She just had to get these other briquettes. Fine. Well, I'm not going to let this ruin our dinner time. I can still salvage this situation. I'll finish cooking these carcasses and then cut off the burned parts.* So, I left the burners on low, satisfied myself everything was under control, put down the lid, and went back inside.

As I walked back inside I glanced a leery look over my shoulder. Yikes! Once again those demon-possessed flames were gnawing away at the flesh of our poor little chickens! I raced back again and stood there for the next fifteen minutes spraying water on the briquettes every time one of those toady tongues of fire darted up. It was a losing proposition. By the time I finally placed the corpses of those poor chickens on a plate it looked like we were having cremated cat for dinner. They were burned beyond recognition.

I was muttering before I got the door closed. "I can't believe you bought these stupid briquettes. I told you I had carefully considered all three types. Did you think I would intentionally buy the wrong kind of briquettes? Do I look that stupid? Why couldn't you just trust me? Why couldn't you leave well enough alone? Look at these chickens! There's no way we can eat these things! You've ruined our dinner!" Things sort of went downhill from there. Patsy ended up skipping dinner and going to bed early. The kids ate hurriedly, then went in different directions. Boy, can I be a jerk.

After kissing the bride, both husband and wife walk up the wedding aisle into marriage with a broad range of different ideas about raising children, money, sex, being late, sharing household chores, and a zillion other matters—large and small—which lead to conflict.

Husbands tend to deal with conflict in one or more of four different ways. They tend to *avoid, explode, perpetuate*, or *resolve* conflict. Let's look briefly at each of these responses. And keep in mind that these can just as easily apply to wives.

AVOID

Why do some husbands try to avoid conflict? Actually, it's best to avoid conflict when we can. Some men, however, prefer to avoid conflict at all costs.

The perfectionist husband pictures himself above getting angry. He doesn't believe a truly spiritual man should ever be upset but should have perfect control over himself. After all, if he is walking in the Spirit then everything should be perfect.

I believe many Christian men are a whole lot angrier than they would dare imagine.

I believe many Christian men are a whole lot angrier than they would dare imagine. We believe anger is a sin (it is not—losing control is), and so we suppress it.

On Friday mornings I rise at 4:00 A.M. to finish preparing to teach a Bible study at 7:00 A.M. I need this time to really be properly prepared. One Thursday night not long ago I became furiously angry, but I wasn't about to ruin my testimony for the next morning. Instead of dealing constructively with my anger, I chose to pretend it wasn't there. So I set my alarm and went to bed, but I was steamed.

The next morning I woke up startled at 6:00 A.M. I blinked and squinted at the dial on the alarm clock. *This can't be happening!* I checked another clock. *6:00 A.M.* Then I checked the alarm. It was set to go off at 8:00 A.M.

My anger the night before caused me to miss setting the alarm to the right time by four hours! I rushed around and made it to our Bible study on time, but I'll never forget the lesson—we need to deal with our upset feelings. There are practical consequences of not dealing constructively with anger or even denying we are angry at all. The New Testament teaches, "Do not let the sun go down while you are still angry, and do not give the devil a foothold" (Ephesians 4:26–27).

Many husbands do not know how to constructively express their anger. In *Healing for Damaged Emotions* David Seamands says,

> Be angry, but be careful. Anger becomes resentful and bitter when you don't know proper ways to express it. This is exactly what happens to the perfectionist who can never even allow himself to express anger; who won't even allow himself to be aware that he is angry. He denies

it and pushes it down deep into his inner self where it simmers and festers and comes out in various kinds of disguised emotional problems, marital conflicts, and even in forms of physical illness.[1]

Being timid, another way to avoid conflict, shows up in the husband who is insecure about himself. Perhaps he married a strong-willed woman or simply a woman who has a mind of her own. She may respond to differences of opinion in angry outbursts or by pouting. To keep the peace he tries to grin and bear it and so suppresses his anger.

One secret of our marriage is that we know each other's hot buttons, but we have agreed not to push them.

Then there is the husband who has learned how to avoid conflict constructively. He has mastered the art of letting the little ones go (see Proverbs 19:11). He seeks to make bigger and bigger offenses seem smaller and smaller. When he does speak, he tries not to criticize or offer unwanted advice by making statements like, "Let me tell you what you need to do."

A man married for forty-six years told me, "One secret of our marriage is that we know each other's hot buttons, but we have agreed not to push them." A husband like this should be encouraged and commended.

EXPLODE

Sometimes the accumulated pressures get to husbands and we blow up. Unfortunately, rather than constructively expressing feelings of anger, we often lose our tempers. This, of course, is horrible, and here is how it happens.

First, there is the husband with a short fuse. His problem is the frequency with which he flares up in anger. He shows no hesitation to upset the family climate. He raises the temperature at the dinner table without thinking. He doesn't seem to care that he ruins the family peace. Often, he gets overly upset by what should be minor irritations.

Certain cultures and certain temperaments seem to actually enjoy arguing. Tim LaHaye points out in *Understanding the Male Temperament* that hard-driving Type A personalities ("cholerics") can use angry outbursts as a weapon to get their own way. He says, "His wife is usually afraid of him, and he tends to terrify his children."[2] Marriage counselor Gary Smalley notes that most women are afraid of their husbands. My own informal surveys agree.

Another type of husband doesn't get angry often, but when he does, watch out! He loses control. His problem is the intensity of his anger. He does okay for a while but eventually things build up and it finally gets to him.

The exploder causes conflict inside his home because he doesn't have the courage to resolve his conflict outside the home.

Why does a husband explode? He is angry at work, but he suppresses it. He is angry at inconsiderate drivers, but he suppresses it. He is angry because his friend didn't show up for tennis, but he suppresses it. He is angry because his paycheck doesn't go far enough, but he suppresses it. Finally, he erupts at his wife because he can't suppress it any longer.

Judy served a beautiful dinner. The rice, however, wasn't hot enough to melt the butter. Rick blew up, acting as if his wife had secretly laced the food with strychnine ... a thought that has occurred to her.

The exploder causes conflict inside his home because he doesn't have the courage to resolve his conflict outside the home. He responds to a light accidentally left on with the rage accumulated from a boss who took credit for an idea, a raise that didn't happen, and a near miss on the highway that made him slam on the brakes.

Exploders can be cruel, cutting, and sarcastic. Their wives will occasionally shiver at how cold they can be, as though these men have ice water running through their veins.

The man who explodes at his wife acts with immaturity. He sins against her, and he must learn to control himself.

PERPETUATE

Some husbands perpetuate conflict by childishly holding grudges, and a few of them even have a mean streak.

The husband who holds grudges against his wife has trouble letting things go. He has stockpiled munitions and rations to last through a long, bitter struggle. His is a duration problem. His stubborn pride won't let him back down or admit he might be wrong. Husbands who hold grudges put a lot of pressure on their families.

Then there is the husband who walks around under a black cloud of negativity. He could find fault with Mother Teresa. This husband tends by temperament to be negative, pessimistic, and critical. He is self-centered, thin-skinned, and touchy. He tends to be revengeful and persecution-prone. He may be legalistic and rigid. As a result he tends to keep past grievances simmering on the back burner, useful ammunition to bring up during future fights.

Another type of perpetuator doesn't enjoy starting conflicts, but he never backs down once a conflict breaks out. He always has to get in the last word. He fights fire with gasoline. The only thing that brings him to his senses are his wife's tears as she bursts out sobbing.

Sometimes husbands can be overly obstinate. One wife told me, "My husband doesn't believe in giving birthday cards and gifts. He thinks expensive cards are a rip-off. He has agreed that I can buy him birthday cards if I want to, and I do. But in over twenty years of marriage he has never given me a card." Later in the conversation she added, "There are some areas in our marriage we just don't talk about." I guess not.

All husbands sometimes have a hard time admitting that they may be wrong. Some husbands, however, cannot brook the thought of ever being wrong.

RESOLVE

Some husbands face their conflicts head on and heal relationships. This type of husband understands himself and has committed to walk in the Spirit, not gratifying the desires of his sinful nature.

My wife's grandfather was once the chief operating officer of Monsanto, the large chemical company. Four beautiful Chippendale chairs graced his office over the years.

For many years Patsy's parents decorated their home with these artful, sacred chairs. When they downsized their home they asked if we would like them. I leaped!

Imagine the important conversations upon which those chairs have eavesdropped! What secrets they must hide in that dark-grained wood. The historicity, the nostalgia, the sentimentality. I love that kind of stuff.

Shortly after we brought the chairs into our home I priced a needed reupholstering job. I had no idea decent fabric could cost so much! For the time being the chairs would have to go in a storage closet.

For over a year I dreamed of those historic, Martha Washington-style Chippendale chairs adorning my office. In my mind I had seen these rejuvenated chairs delivered by the reupholsterer and arced around my desk. For several months I knew I had a big paycheck on the way. Without discussing it with Patsy, I planned to redo the chairs when the money came in.

A day or two before the check was to arrive I made a small side comment that I wanted to get the chairs redone. Patsy immediately seized the moment and said, "I disagree. I think we should use the money to build up our reserves."

Now, what I felt like doing was to scream, holler, and yell. I wanted to pout. I wanted to rant and rave. But the moment the words left her lips I knew she was right. This happened on one of my better days, and so I responded with maturity and we resolved the conflict. The graceful grain of those heirloom chairs will have to wait for another day.

As men, our reactions to minor irritations are often way out of proportion to the perceived "offense." "Misdemeanors" get treated like "felonies."

It takes a great deal of courage to resolve conflict head on. Most men find it easier to bottle up their work frustrations than deal with them. Then later, we blow. As men, our reactions to minor irritations are often way out of proportion to the perceived "offense." "Misdemeanors" get treated like "felonies." Those occasions trigger pent up frustrations. We act toward our wives in ways we would never act toward coworkers or, for that matter, perfect strangers.

As your husbands we want you to know that we are sorry. We really do have it in our hearts to resolve our conflicts with more maturity.

BIBLICAL PRINCIPLES FOR MANAGING CONFLICTS IN MARRIAGE

This is a book to help you understand what your husband is like, what he's going through, and why he does the things he does. However, conflict management and resolution is such an important area that I am taking the extra step in this chapter to offer some biblical ideas I first mentioned in *Devotions for Couples* (formerly titled *Two Part Harmony*) that you and your husband can reflect upon and practice. They can be a great aid to avoiding and resolving the inevitable conflicts that every couple has.

Obviously, the objective should be to avoid conflicts when possible and resolve them biblically when you can't.

Overlook offenses. Try to let offenses go when you can. "A man's wisdom gives him patience; it is to his glory to overlook an offense" (Proverbs 19:11).

Remain calm. No matter how relaxed you are normally, everyone occasionally gets upset. If your spouse gets rattled, try to stay calm. If you don't respond in kind, the matter may simply go away. "If a ruler's anger rises against you, do not leave your post; calmness can lay great errors to rest" (Ecclesiastes 10:4).

> *Listen carefully to what your mate is really trying to say. Many conflicts happen because we didn't really "hear" what was said.*

Don't respond too quickly. Listen carefully to what your mate is really trying to say. Many conflicts happen because we didn't really "hear" what was said. Ask lots of questions to understand the "real" problem. Try to never respond from a strictly emotional state. The old "count to ten" adage is an adage for good reason. Cool down and add reason to your response. "My dear brothers, take note of this: Everyone should be quick to listen, slow to speak and slow to become angry" (James 1:19).

Do not speak recklessly. Hurtful words are like poison-tipped arrows that have left the archer's bow: Once they are in the air they cannot be retrieved. Let go too often and they can destroy a relationship. "Reckless words pierce like a sword, but the tongue of the wise brings healing" (Proverbs 12:18).

Do not escalate the conflict. When you do have conflicts with each other, try to work through them as a couple. Don't involve others in your quarrels in the heat of the moment. Later, if the conflict remains unresolved you may want outside help, but give it some time. "He who covers over an offense promotes love, but whoever repeats the matter separates close friends" (Proverbs 17:9).

Do not say everything that comes to mind. A lot of arguments and quarrels escalate because we keep saying those clever, razor-edged zingers that come to mind. Bite your tongue—the Bible calls it "a restless evil, full of deadly poison" (James 3:8). "Without wood a fire goes out; without gossip a quarrel dies down" (Proverbs 26:20).

> *Hurtful words are like poison-tipped arrows that have left the archer's bow: Once they are in the air they cannot be retrieved.*

Trust the Lord will solve your conflicts. Not every conflict will be resolved the way you want. The question is: Could you be wrong? The best approach is to turn to God and ask him to put the burden of reconciliation on your spouse's heart or show you where you have erred. "Do not say, 'I'll pay you back for this wrong!' Wait for the LORD, and he will deliver you" (Proverbs 20:22).[3]

HOW YOU CAN HELP YOUR HUSBAND

- Take a moment and put your marriage conflicts in perspective. As a couple do you fuss a lot, too much, not that often, or hardly ever?
- Who is primarily responsible for your conflicts—you, your husband, 50/50, or some other split?
- Of the four ways husbands respond to conflict, which ones best describe your husband? Which ones describe you?

- All things considered, how big of a problem do you have?
- Which of the principles for managing conflict in marriage does your husband need to apply better? How about you?

This is such an important area. If it seems appropriate, why not suggest to your husband that he read this chapter. Then set aside thirty minutes or so to discuss it after the kids are in bed. During this time tell your husband how you answered the questions just posed in this section, diplomatically, but with candor. Use that time to renew your commitments to each other.

A THOUGHT FOR HUSBANDS

Marriage means conflict. It's unavoidable. The issue is not how to avoid conflict but how to constructively handle the inevitable conflicts we will have over raising children, money, sex, being late, sharing household chores, and a zillion other large and small matters.

In this chapter I have shown your wife how we husbands tend to handle conflicts by *avoiding, exploding, perpetuating,* or *resolving* them. To learn more about these responses you may want to also read the corresponding subheading in this chapter.

In the section "How You Can Help Your Husband" I asked your wife to consider some questions. Here they are again for you to consider too:

- Take a moment and put your marriage conflicts in perspective. As a couple do you fuss a lot, too much, not that often, or hardly ever?
- Of the four ways men respond to conflict (avoid, explode, perpetuate, resolve), which ones best describe you? Which ones describe your wife?

- Who is primarily responsible for your conflicts—you, your wife, 50/50, or some other split?
- All things considered, how big of a problem do you have?
- Under the heading "Biblical Principles for Managing Conflicts in Marriage," seven principles for managing and resolving conflict are mentioned. Which of the principles does your wife need to apply better? How about you?

It takes a great deal of courage to resolve conflict head on. Many of us find it easier to bottle up our frustrations than to deal with them. But later, we blow up over the silliest things.

In this chapter I told your wife, "As your husbands we want you to know that we are sorry. We really do have it in our hearts to resolve our conflicts with more maturity." Why not express that to her in your own words.

Eleven ∾

*A*ppearance
Why a Man Wants His Wife
to Look Good

*E*very woman is beautiful in her own way. It may be the fleeting beauty of her physical appearance—even if a single characteristic like her eyes. Perhaps it's the unfading beauty of a gentle and quiet spirit. Maybe it's the loving way she is with her family, friends, or hurting people.

In this chapter I want to pass along some things you ought to know. Let me digress and remind you that I'm writing in such a way that your husband could read this book and say, "Yes, he's articulating what I'm feeling. Honey, would you read this book so you'll understand me better?"

HOW NORMAL MEN FEEL

I informally polled over 150 men about how important they assess the physical appearance of their wives. The three choices were, "not important, somewhat important, very important."

While 95 percent of the same group (on a different day) said sex is a "major issue" to them, over 95 percent responded that physical appearance is "somewhat important." No man

171

responded "not important." Only a handful responded "very important."

What a man hopes for is that his wife will portray a certain dignity in her looks that is consistent with his image of himself.

A typical husband wants his wife to look good, but he is not obsessed. However, he does consider his wife's appearance a reflection on *his* judgment. A man wants to feel proud of his wife.

What a man hopes for is that his wife will portray a certain dignity in her looks that is consistent with his image of *himself.*

Husbands vary, of course, but they are interested in the way their wives dress, their weight, and personal grooming including makeup and hair. Within the family budget he wants his wife to take good care of her appearance.

What first attracted him to his wife was her looks, and they are still important to him. Read the following sentence I'm writing twice and note the changed emphasis.

Your husband wants to *stay* married to the woman who attracted him.

Your husband wants to stay married to the woman who *attracted* him.

If I picked up anything during the research for this book it is that husbands want to stay married. They also want you to continue "attracting" them.

Our family once visited the Miami Zoo. As we walked along, I remember passing a young mother with two children, one a toddler, the other in a stroller. Instantly I knew that she was not married. I knew because of the way she dressed. She was dressed to "attract." I might add she did so in a dignified way, but it was still obvious.

If any wife reading this book could say, "If my husband died, after my mourning time I would lose thirty pounds, fix my hair a new way, and buy a new wardrobe," she can be almost certain of this: Her husband secretly wishes she would go ahead and do it now.

Here's the point: Men don't stop caring about "attraction."

A BEAUTY-BASED CULTURE

After teaching the "Finding a New Best Friend and Supporter in Your Wife" session in our men's seminar, a man waited until everyone else had left, then asked if we could talk. He said, "I love my wife so much. I really want to be a godly husband. But my wife has gained forty pounds since we married. I've tried to talk to her about it, but she immediately gets defensive. When I bring it up she takes it to mean I don't love her unconditionally." At this point tears started down his cheeks and he added, "This is a real issue to me. I just don't know what to do."

We live in a youth-centered, beauty-based, sex-oriented society. I do not think it is possible for a husband to fully separate himself from the values of his culture. Some cultures, of course, don't put a premium on weight.

A lovely African-American woman who is a friend of our family decided to lose forty pounds. She did, and she looks super. However, her culture values, even prizes, "plump." Family and friends ribbed her, "Girl, you look sick! You're too skinny. You're gonna' shrivel up and die!"

One of my pastors returned not long ago from a trip to Romania. He said, "Everyone over thirty-five years old was thirty to forty pounds overweight." But a friend who returned from the Far East commented, "You don't see any fat Orientals."

What do husbands think they should reasonably be able to expect? Every population segment has a culture that values,

Every population segment has a culture that values, even sanctions, acceptable and desirable forms of physical appearance. Husbands want their wives to "fit in" with their group.

even sanctions, acceptable and desirable forms of physical appearance. Husbands want their wives to "fit in" with their group.

What's fair for a husband to ask of his wife?

TRUE BEAUTY

A college student at our church brought home a lovely young lady he's dating. While she was talking to my wife I said to him, "She's a very beautiful person."

He brightened and said, "And she's just as beautiful on the inside as she is on the outside!" He was making a profound point.

What do men consider true beauty? Most men can differentiate between outward and inward beauty. The Bible offers clear thinking about this difference.

The Bible is full of beautiful women. Sarah, Rebekah, Rachel, Abigail, Bathsheba, Esther, and Job's daughters are all described as beautiful women.

Their outward beauty, however, was a manifestation of their inner beauty. A fascinating passage of the New Testament discloses the secret of their beauty and the true beauty of women in all generations.

Your beauty should not come from outward adornment, such as braided hair and the wearing of gold jewelry and fine clothes. Instead, it *should be that of your inner self, the unfading beauty of a gentle and quiet spirit,* which is of great worth in God's sight. *For this is the way the holy women of the past who put their hope in God used to make themselves beautiful.* They were submissive to their own husbands, *like Sarah,* who obeyed Abraham and called him her master. *You are her daughters if you do what is right and do not give way to fear* (1 Peter 3:3–6, emphasis added).

In other words, the beauty of these women of the Bible was an outward expression of their inner person, a reflection of the unfading beauty of a gentle and quiet spirit.

Wives become "daughters of Sarah" by pursuing this inner beauty: "You are her daughters if you do what is right and do not give way to fear."

It is worth noting that the Bible does not prohibit outward adornment. John Calvin put it this way, "It would be immoderate strictness simply to forbid neatness and elegance in clothing."

Men appreciate wives who "adorn" themselves to remain attractive, but they may or may not understand it is merely a means to feature a woman's inward beauty. Physical beauty is fleeting (Proverbs 31:30), and in a sex-saturated society husbands sometimes need to be reminded to hold realistic expectations.

God created us—men and women—to observe beauty (see Genesis 2:9). We feel pleasure in observing great expanses of nature, the eye-catching symmetry of a manicured landscape, and the greatest of all achievements—the human body.

If I took all the beautiful women I've ever known and grouped them by decades, the loveliest is in the last half of her "seventies" decade. Her radiant countenance is legendary around our church. Where does this beauty come from? Knowing her, it is clear that her beauty is the outward expression of the unfading beauty of a gentle and quiet spirit.

WHAT'S FAIR

What should husbands and wives be able to expect from each other in the area of physical appearance? What is fair, reasonable, and balanced? I would like to suggest for your consideration the following idea: A husband should be able to expect his wife to work at remaining as physically attractive as she was when they married, reasonably proportioned to the years gone by.

A husband should be able to expect his wife to work at remaining as physically attractive as she was when they married, reasonably proportioned to the years gone by.

A wife should be able to expect her husband to work at nurturing her inner person so that she matures to the unfading beauty of a gentle and quiet spirit.

For the majority of our culture it seems okay for men to gain weight as the years roll by, but not for women. Expectations of husbands in this area must be carefully and lovingly balanced against the laws of nature. Above all, under no circumstances is it fair for either spouse to hold their mate to a standard they themselves are not willing to keep.

HOW YOU CAN HELP YOUR HUSBAND

Be willing to dress for your husband. Every woman chooses, consciously or not, to maintain her appearance for one of five *primary* audiences:

- Her husband
- Her peers
- Other men
- Herself
- No one (she doesn't care about her appearance)

If your husband feels you are not sensitive to him as your primary audience, you have a problem. I realize that this topic is sensitive. In fact, it is so sensitive that to ignore this issue, or to be so upset that you don't deal constructively with it, is to risk a downward spiral.

First, the wife lets her appearance slip (assuming he does not). Her husband attempts to talk to her about it. It becomes a sore spot. He stops bringing it up.

I believe after a few rejected attempts at communication on this, a husband will no longer be able to muster the courage to tell his wife exactly how he feels about her appearance if she will

A wife should be able to expect her husband to work at nurturing her inner person so that she matures to the unfading beauty of a gentle and quiet spirit.

not (1) make him the primary audience for her appearance and (2) work at remaining as physically attractive as she was when they married, reasonably proportioned to the years gone by.

Though he stops bringing it up, the issue hasn't gone away. He later stops saying nice things about her appearance. His romantic interest wanes. Her emotional bank account goes empty. An emotional distance develops between them. They coexist.

Be willing to "hear" your husband, especially if you hear repetitive mentions of issues. If you sense from your husband a lack of romantic interest, looks, and physical touch, consider your appearance.

Be willing to make appropriate changes. When we married, Patsy simply would not go and buy new clothes. Finally, I took her shopping one day and she purchased some very useful things. Over the years she learned that her appearance was important to me. She realized that when she dressed with dignity it made me feel proud inside to be her husband. All men want this.

In return, I am working to be more of a nurturer. I realize that to be a truly beautiful person, Patsy must receive something from me. Only then will she attain that beauty "of [her] inner self, the unfading beauty of a gentle and quiet spirit."

A THOUGHT FOR HUSBANDS

Every woman is beautiful in her own way." Do you agree or disagree, and why?

The appearance of our wives is important to us because we want to feel proud of our women.

At the same time, we must distinguish between the outward appearance of "fleeting beauty" (Proverbs 31:30) and "the unfading beauty of a gentle and quiet spirit" (1 Peter 3:4). How does a wife attain this inner beauty?

Bill McCartney, founder of Promise Keepers and former head coach of the University of Colorado national champion football team, once heard a visiting preacher say, "You can tell the depth of a man's walk with God by looking at the countenance of his wife's face."

Tendency: To care about how our wife looks, but not have a clue about how to nurture her inner person.

McCartney says he turned and looked at that moment into his wife's eyes and realized that he had neglected the nurture of his beloved wife. Not long after he resigned as the head coach at Colorado. Most people assumed it was to devote more time to Promise Keepers. Actually, he wanted to reconnect with his wife and was fortunate enough financially that he could take some time off.

Our wives attain "the unfading beauty of a gentle and quiet spirit" when we nurture, love, and cherish them.

What are the reasonable expectations we should have of our wives, and them of us? In this chapter two complementary ideas were proposed. Do these seem fair to you?

- A husband should be able to expect his wife to work at remaining as physically attractive as she was when they married, reasonably proportioned to the years gone by.
- A wife should be able to expect her husband to work at nurturing her inner person so that she matures to the unfading beauty of a gentle and quiet spirit.

What have your expectations been? Have they been reasonable and realistic? How should you amend your thinking?

Challenge: Care more about your wife's inner person than her outward appearance.

Caution: No husband should expect to hold his wife's appearance to a standard he himself is not willing to meet. No husband should make his love and acceptance of his wife conditional upon her appearance.

Tendency: To care about how our wife looks, but not have a clue about how to nurture her inner person.

Challenge: Care more about your wife's inner person than her outward appearance.

Twelve ❧

Fathering
Your Husband's Changing View
of Being a Dad

After a heated argument, Larry's nineteen-year-old son stormed to his room and packed his things to leave home.

His father met him at the front door and said, "You're not going to leave mad. We're going to sit down and talk this out. If you still want to leave after that I'll support you, but you're not going to leave mad."

By talking things out they were able to work through their differences. When the conversation ended Larry's son embraced him with both arms, having decided to stay.

Something that happened to Larry when he himself was eighteen makes this story especially poignant. His parents met him at the front door one evening as he was leaving to see his girlfriend. They blocked the door and issued an ultimatum: "You're going to have to stop seeing that girl or find another place to live."

"But Mom and Dad, you're not giving me any choice!" They argued back and forth, but Larry's parents wouldn't budge. That night, when he walked out the front door, Larry moved away from home and never returned. That was twenty-five years ago. He became a pastor and married the girl he was on his way to see that night. She is the mother of the son he met at his own front door.

Larry has been able to reestablish contact with his parents in recent years, but that horrible incident has never been mentioned. It's interesting how certain decisions—some made hastily, some seeming small at the time—can completely alter the course of our lives.

THE HEART OF FATHERS

$\mathcal{F}$athers exert an overpowering influence on their kids. Fathering is a noble task, and most fathers have noble motives, yet many fall short of their own expectations. Nevertheless, most men have it in their hearts to be like their own good father, or the good father they never had.

Fathers in every generation have always wanted the best for their children. How to bring that about has changed. The role of the father is changing quickly in our culture. Often, today's father is doing the opposite of his father before him.

Most men have it in their hearts to be like their own good father, or the good father they never had.

From our research and seminars we know that many men have had little training on how to be a good dad. A grocery store executive left his wife and children, later went back, but eventually left his family for good. He said, "You know, I don't get it. I have received all kinds of training. I've been trained in handling money. I've been trained how to do my work. I've been trained how to be an executive. But no one ever trained me how to be a husband and father. Where does a man go to get that kind of training? I guess it's too late for me, but what about the other men out there like me? What are they supposed to do?"

BIBLICAL FATHERING

Surprisingly, while the Bible tells us what a good father should do, it gives few examples of highly involved, successful fathers.

On the other hand, the Bible records a number of examples of underinvolved fathering. For example, "When Samuel grew old ... his sons did not walk in his ways. They turned aside after dishonest gain and accepted bribes and perverted justice" (1 Samuel 8:1, 3).

Samuel was the prophet who anointed David king of Israel. How could such a great prophet have such sorry sons?

To understand, we must look back to his own boyhood. Samuel's mother sent him to live in the temple with Eli. Eli had two sons, but they were wicked. They slept with women near the entrance of the temple and did many other contemptible things. Eli didn't pay attention to his sons' behavior until he was old. Even then, he didn't correct their bad behavior.

So the only role model Samuel had was Eli, and as a dad Eli was a "dud." When Samuel became a man he emulated Eli's "hands-off fathering" approach, and his own sons became just as wicked as Eli's sons. Pretty pathetic, isn't it?

It is fascinating that almost every detailed example of fathering in the Bible is one of failure, not success. Adam had problems with Cain and Abel. Abraham had problems with Isaac and Ishmael. Isaac had problems with Jacob and Esau. Jacob had problems when his sons sold their brother Joseph into slavery.

David, too, had his fill of troubles. His son Amnon raped Tamar, his half sister and David's daughter. David's son Absalom then killed Amnon. Absalom also attempted to overthrow his father. So did another of David's sons, Adonijah. Absalom was killed by David's general. Adonijah was assassinated by David's son Solomon. It's not a pretty picture.

In one sense, the fact that these godly men had sons who turned out badly should be a comfort to some men. A child can accidentally turn out wrong.

On the other hand, because of God's grace, many young people come to love God even though their fathers don't.

Fathering principles have changed dramatically, especially in this generation. Let's explore how fathering has been shifting.

THE ABSENT FATHER

The last generation of fathers grew up in the era of Wilson Sloan's *Man in the Gray Flannel Suit*. These nomadic corporate ladder climbers were sons of the industrial revolution.

Our fathers were often stoic because that's the example set for them. They tended not to be relational. They usually avoided physical affection. They often didn't express verbal affection with words like, "I love you." Dad was proud of us, but he tended to withhold expressions of approval and unconditional acceptance. Some of our dads were very strict, while others became part of the "permissive parent" generation. In either case, it was not easy to get close to dad.

Dad was proud of us, but he tended to withhold expressions of approval and unconditional acceptance.

Father's first loyalty was to his company, mainly because the company demanded first priority in a man's life. Large corporations moved their men regularly, and strict obedience was expected.

In 1900 over half of America's population lived in farming communities.[1] In farming families the father was a visible factor around the home. As the industrial revolution emerged, fathers were removed from the full-orbed daily life of the family to specialized factory or office jobs.

Men left early in the morning and were not seen again until the end of the day. Some observers believe the effect on the family was devastating. If nothing else, it's a good reminder that the culture of "the absent father" is a recent phenomenon in history.

In the 1950s and 1960s the roles of mother and father were well defined. Mom was the "hands-on" parent who expressed love; dad was the "hands-off" parent who made the money. Often, he held down two jobs. Between his time commitments and values, dad wasn't part of the PTA. He wasn't a coach for his son's little league team. He didn't drive his daughters to soccer practice—they didn't even play soccer!

Men increasingly consider corporate loyalty a thing to be balanced against family needs.

TODAY'S NEW FATHER

If our dads were the sons of the industrial age, we are the sons of the information age.

The pendulum is swinging. Fathering has shifted from "hands-off" to "hands-on." Today's father tends to be more relational, more verbal, more of a hugger, and spends more time with his kids.

Many of today's new fathers see the relationship between career and family differently than their dads did. Men increasingly consider corporate loyalty a thing to be balanced against family needs. Today, men are saying, "I want to have more balance in my priorities—I want to be there for my kids." All in all, a profound change has taken place in men's attitudes.

Men today remain removed from much of the daily life of the family because of the physical locations of their work, but dads today place greater emphasis on balancing the need for money with the need for daddy.

One father, a partner in a national accounting firm, told his company in the early 1970s that he was not going to move again. At the time his two children were entering middle school. Within a few short years he was no longer employed there. It was, "move around and move up, or move out." But he has no regrets. "I wanted to put down my roots and stay. That's what I did, and things have worked out." While this type of corporate thinking still exists, things are changing—if slowly.

In the late 1980s an executive with a major oil company was asked to "move up" and take a promotion. That meant uprooting his kids from their schools and friends and his wife from her neighborhood and friends, and they would have to leave their church. He declined the promotion, and several more over the next few years. Eventually, they stopped asking, but his company realized they had an extremely loyal, valuable employee and he is still with them.

Company attitudes are changing today to make room for men who want to make greater commitments to family priorities. Yet, many companies still run things the same old way. Recently I sat next to a man on a plane on his way to interview with a potential employer. His existing company was asking him to move for the fourth time in five years!

It's encouraging to see how many fathers today act with leadership and stick up for a more balanced set of fathering principles.

PRINCIPLES OF HANDS-ON FATHERING

The Involved Father

The biggest change in hands-on fathering is the amount of time fathers want to spend with their kids. And it's not just the time they spend, but what they are willing to give up or adjust to spend it. I serve on a board with men from around the country. At a recent two-day board meeting a man said good-bye to me at the end of the first day. I said, "Where are you going?"

There is a growing sense among fathers that they want to "be there" for the momentous occasions in the lives of their children.

"I'm going home so I can attend my daughter's sixth-grade commencement tomorrow."

I must have raised my eyebrows because he added, "I know it doesn't sound like that big of a deal, but it's a really big deal to her." As an afterthought he added, "I will say my wife had to urge me to come back for it."

What a beautiful illustration of a father "in process." A willing heart. An encouraging wife. A happy daughter. Of course, some meetings must be attended. But there is a growing sense among fathers that they want to "be there" for the momentous occasions in the lives of their children.

We teach men in our seminars, "If you don't have enough time for your children you can be 100 percent certain that you are not following God's will for your life." I've never had a father disagree.

Every man I know would be willing to die for his children. More and more, men are willing to live for them too.

The Balanced Father

Another big change in hands-on fathering is the move from *law* to *grace*. Perhaps Jim Dobson's famous idea sums it up: "Growing up is difficult. Our job should be to just help them get through it."

Two great problems of fathering are (1) a lack of structure and (2) too much structure. The biblical fathers already mentioned are examples of fathers who didn't provide enough structure. Often the problem is the opposite—too much structure. The children see dad as a strict, rigid disciplinarian detached from the "daily" part of family life. Like an eagle perched high above, dad remains aloof until the children need to be disciplined. Then he swoops down, slaps the kids around, and returns to his perch until he's needed again. As one man said, "No matter what I did, I could never please my father."

Every man I know would be willing to die for his children. More and more, men are willing to live for them too.

In our seminars we teach fathers, "You can raise your children under grace or law, but grace is better. If you raise them under law they may not want to spend much time with you once they are on their own."

The tendency of fathers is to provide too much structure where there should be freedom, and too much freedom where there should be structure. For example, fathers often have many strict rules about the physical appearance of their teenagers, but don't ask enough questions about what kind of company they keep.

Hands-on fathers realize their children need more grace. They want to encourage and not discourage their kids.

The Expressive Father

Another principle of hands-on fathering is the effort to be more expressive, both verbally and physically.

One day when my son, John, was thirteen he said, "Dad, would you rebound for me?" I've never wanted anything in my life as much as John wanted basketball. He ate it up. He practiced without ceasing.

I was elated to be asked and said, "Sure." He lofted up a ball and it went *swishhhh*. I said, "Great shot, John. Great shot."

He fired up another one. It bricked off the side of the rim. "Remember how you said you wanted to keep your elbow straight. I think it might have been a little crooked on that one."

He let go another shot. It rattled around the rim then dropped through the hoop. "Super, John. You're looking good."

John stopped dribbling, looked at me, and said, "Dad, would you please not try to coach me."

To be honest, tears came to my eyes. This was not the first time something like this had happened. I was trying to do something positive—trying to make an investment in my son. But it was turning out all wrong.

As I began to make a reply I believe God gave me an insight. I said, "John, I know that I can't coach you, but I love you very much and only want the best for you. I'm not trying to coach you—I know I'm not qualified to do that. Son, I'm trying to *encourage* you."

Sonic *booooom!* He understood. I understood. There's a difference between trying to be a cheerleader and a coach! In that suspended instant father and son connected. The skies parted. Light broke through. It was a Kodak moment.

Then he added, "Dad, I'd still appreciate it if you wouldn't say anything when I'm shooting."

Dads often struggle with expressing physical affection. Studies from the '70s showed that most parents only touched their children out of necessity, like helping them dress or getting into the car.[2] Today's father is at least hearing more about physical affection, and many are taking it to heart.

Today's father wants to be more of a hugger and encourager. Fathers are realizing they need to tell their children, "I love you" and "I'm proud of you."

THE MYTH OF THE SUPER DAD

A survey conducted by the National Center for Fathering among Promise Keepers attendees (largely a group of active churchmen) asked men to respond to the statement, "Being a father is overwhelming." Forty-one percent said this statement is, "mostly true or somewhat true."[3]

Many fathers, especially younger ones, feel overwhelmed trying to juggle all that's expected of the "twenty-first century" father. These husbands and fathers tell me they feel society now expects them to be a loving and attentive father who participates in all their children's activities, a talkative and touching husband who spends gobs of time with his wife and pitches in around the house, an active layman who gets involved in the ministries of the church, and a successful (read "making plenty of money") worker who finances a "brand names only" lifestyle.

Several years ago a man from Texas, frustrated with the way his life was turning out, made some major changes in his life. He started a men's study group for other men going through similar struggles. He found the response was tremendous, and he still leads the group today.

In a recent letter he eloquently framed the frustration many men are feeling. Let's pick it up after the opening paragraphs.

> What is frustrating, though, is that as I look back at my life and the lives of the men involved [in his group], I see very little change. When I look at that original roster of fourteen men, a few left their wives, a few got a great promotion and are working more now than ever, some have dropped out from lack of interest, etc.
>
> I find the same situation happening in other men's ministries. When thirty of us came home from a men's

retreat a few years ago we were filled with excitement. But within a few weeks, we were back in our same ruts as before.

I have spent a great deal of time pondering this situation. While there are many reasons involved, I find the relationship with our wives most interesting. The wives of the guys in my group and those who went on the retreat seem very supportive. They are excited about the possibility that their husbands might make marriage a bigger priority. Or spend more time with their kids. Or be more of a spiritual leader. Or spend less time at the office. The problem is that *it takes time to do all these things!*

I used to work sixty hours a week. Now I barely hit forty. And I am very pleased because I have gotten more joy than ever before from being with my kids. My marriage is better than ever. I am more balanced than ever before. But my wife still would like a new car next year and there is no money at all for that. And my kids would like brand-name clothes, just like everyone else has. And all the other families are going to Disney World ... why can't we?

I talk about this situation with guys. When you and your wife are "visualizing" all these benefits, are you also visualizing yourself in a twelve-year-old car in the church parking lot with a hubcap missing and a dead battery? Will your wife still be excited about things then? To be honest, don't most wives want the good things in life? And don't they also want their husbands to be very involved in the family life? I don't know about you, but I can't earn $70,000 a year working forty hours a week.

For many of us, creating the time required to be a great father, wonderful husband, and involved layperson means a *substantial* reduction in standard of living (and

I'm all for it!). But some of our wives don't understand that. I think a husband and wife need to sit down, *together*, and ask, "Are we willing to reduce our standard of living substantially in order to create this new lifestyle?" If, *together*, we say "yes," then we are *together* in our understanding and much more likely to make it work.

The problem is that most of us don't do it. We just think we will try harder, go to bed later, give up our hobbies, and quit reading the newspaper and we will "squeeze it into our schedule." But it just doesn't happen. Investing in our family's life takes another forty hours a week. (I haven't read a newspaper in a month!)

In the '70s and '80s men had the great misconception that their wives could work full-time, be a great mate, spend endless time with the children, cook extensively, and have time left over. You remember? The "super mom." Well, we now know there is no such thing. Nor is there such a thing as the "super dad." And we men are no more capable of doing it than the women were. But the same women don't know that yet.

Somehow, we need to shed light on this situation to help husbands, wives, and kids come to a better understanding here. I know there is a way, I just haven't got a handle on it yet.

Oops. Got to go. I'm sorry this has been written so haphazardly, but I've got family duties to tend to!

Sincerely,

Carl

The role of the father is changing. In the process of change, husbands need to make sure it is not merely a process of "adding" more things to an already overcommitted schedule.

Husbands must decide to strike a right balance among their competing priorities. Every time he does something, he is *not* doing something else. Wives need to discern how much they can realistically expect their husbands to do, then help them balance all the possibilities.

HOW YOU CAN HELP YOUR HUSBAND

Your husband has probably chosen either the hands-off style of fathering that's on the way out or the hands-on style of fathering that's on the way in.

If your husband is a hands-off father he is, of course, missing a wonderful blessing and an opportunity to mold and shape his children. Pray for him. Encourage him to attend one of the many available men's seminars and conferences. If he is a reader, many titles now address fathering issues.

If your husband is a hands-on father, have you together intentionally decided what adjustments you are willing to make?

Wives need to discern how much they can realistically expect their husbands to do, then help them balance all the possibilities.

Sometimes wives (and husbands) say they want change, but they don't want to give up anything to get it. That's not change! That's trying to have your cake and eat it, too.

If you and your husband find the active, involved, hands-on father an attractive part of your lifestyle, proactively sit down with a calendar and see how to balance the hours between spiritual life, married life, family life, and work life. Decide together what financial and lifestyle sacrifices you would be willing to make to have a greater quality of family life.

And by the way, it might be helpful to encourage your husband when you "catch" him doing something right as a dad.

A THOUGHT FOR HUSBANDS

*F*athers make a unique contribution to the well-being of their kids. No one can influence your children like you can—not moms, preachers, teachers, or coaches. They can help, but fathering is a task that only you can do.

As important as fathering is and as noble as the motives of most fathers are, it is interesting how many of us fall short of our own expectations. Most of us, however, do have it in our hearts to be like our own good father, or the good father we never had.

As the cultural role of the father changes, we often find ourselves doing the exact opposite of our fathers before us.

Fathering is a task that only you can do.

For example, displays of physical affection and regularly saying, "I love you" are common today, but were considerably more rare a generation ago.

While trained for our work, most men haven't had any real training to be a dad. What kind of training have you had to be a good father?

Today's father is moving from hands-off to hands-on. Today we tend to be more relational, more verbal, more of a hugger, and spend more time with our kids than our own dads—largely because of a cultural shift.

Today we often see the relationship between career and family differently than our own dads did. Increasingly we see the need to balance corporate loyalty against family needs. More of us are saying, "I want to have more balance in my priorities—I want to be there for my kids." This is a profound change in our attitudes.

How have your attitudes toward fathering changed? Are you a hands-off or a hands-on father? Take a moment and read the section of the chapter entitled, "The Myth of the Super Dad." How closely do you relate to the issues raised in the letter from Carl in Texas?

Read the section, "Principles of Hands-on Fathering." How involved are you? How balanced? How expressive? If you need to, why not make a move to become a hands-on father?

Why not set a time to talk over your own views about fathering with your wife? Ask her the direction she would like to see the "family time" priority take. What changes would you both be willing to make *together* to bring about the quality of life you desire?

Finally, today there are many wonderful seminars that *do* train fathers how to father. Why not take the initiative to find one and go?

Part Three

Thirteen ❧

Hard Years
Living with a Difficult Husband

One of the things I did to prepare myself to write this book was to teach a series called "What Husbands Wish Their Wives Knew About Men," at our Friday morning Bible study.

One week I told Patsy I would speak on the subject, "Living with a Difficult Husband."

She deadpanned, "Do you want me to come and give a witness?"

As I began the day's lesson I asked the men, "How many of you are, or have been, a difficult husband to live with?"

I could not count the hands, so I asked, "How many of you have *not* been a difficult husband to live with?" Three of the approximately 150 men present raised their hands.

My greatest concern was that men would look around and think, *Well, look at that! That's just the way men are. I'm not that much different. I guess I'm not so bad after all!*

It's not just the average man who struggles. A dozen or so of our ministry leaders were meeting at my home. I asked them, "How many of you are, or have been, a difficult husband to live with?" All but one man raised their hands.

It's a horrible, devastating truth to realize you are a difficult husband. I will never forget the day my wife told me without rancor, "You are a difficult man to live with." It's one thing to vaguely suspect yourself; it's a whole different matter to have the woman you love spell it out for you. Since that time I've strived to improve, and Patsy tells me I have. But it's an easy trap to fall back into.

Wives, we hate ourselves when we are difficult.

A DIFFICULT HUSBAND DEFINED

Not a few wives must live with difficult husbands. These men are browbeaters, manipulators, intimidators, whiners, pouters, grumps, abusers, and neglecters. They may have a biting tongue, or a tongue that rarely responds. They lose their temper or withdraw from family life, or both.

All of us, husbands and wives alike, are difficult to live with from time to time. Occasionally all husbands fall into the trap of browbeating or whining or neglecting or pouting. These are "normal" men. So what's the difference between a "normal" husband who from time to time is difficult and a "difficult" husband who from time to time is normal? It's a line we cross.

All of us, husbands and wives alike, are difficult to live with from time to time.

The truest test of whether a husband is difficult or not is to ask, "Is it chronic?" After repeated, humble attempts by his wife to correct, do the difficulties continue? Does he use *anger* or *withdrawal* as weapons on a *daily* basis?

Another dead giveaway is the "embarrassment test." If a husband would be embarrassed for people to know how he treats his wife, he's difficult. One man put it this way: "If my wife would have repeated some of the things I've done to her, she could have disgraced me."

A husband is difficult if he is one person in public but a dark-sided someone else in private. If a husband isn't living "one life, one way," he may well be a difficult husband.

Difficult husbands can be *verbal* or *nonverbal*. One man yells at his wife. Another man refuses to talk at all.

Difficult husbands can be *aggressive* or *passive*. One man loses his temper. Another whines or pouts.

When we put these four characteristics together we end up with five different kinds of difficult husbands:

1. Browbeaters—Verbal and Aggressive
2. Whiners—Verbal and Passive
3. Neglecters—Nonverbal and Aggressive
4. Pouters—Nonverbal and Passive
5. Abusers—Any of the first four with verbal or physical abuse

Here are some things you ought to know about these five types of difficult husbands.

Browbeaters

At a dinner party in their home, Thomas spent a good two minutes berating his wife in front of their guests because the rolls were not warm.

Scott said, "My style is to come uncorked with only half the facts. On top of that, I overstate the consequences of not doing things my way. I've never seen more than half the facts on any issue because I lose it before I get the whole picture."

Browbeaters are aggressive and verbal. They use their verbal skills to manipulate, intimidate, and criticize. When they lose their tempers they manage to use their superior verbal skill to cut deep into the hearts of their wives. They seem to know all the rights places to carve up.

One irony is that at work browbeaters are often incensed by men who are verbal/aggressive with them or their associates, yet they go right home and do the very same thing to their own wives and children.

Browbeaters often handle big things better than little things. He can lose a big account, learn the refrigerator stopped running, and calmly handle a child caught for experimenting with drugs. But then he will go ballistic when the soap dish falls from a ledge onto the shower floor. What's really happening? In these situations the little things "trigger" the pent-up-but-denied frustration over the big things he appeared to be handling well (but was not). Browbeaters tend to deny anything is wrong on a big scale, then explode over a peccadillo.

Browbeaters tend to deny anything is wrong on a big scale, then explode over a peccadillo.

I'm the answer to Patsy's prayers. I'm not what she prayed for, but I'm the answer she got. I am totally idealistic (a tribute to Plato's "forms"), and I tend to be a perfectionist. I have it so bad that secretly I can't understand why everyone else doesn't want to be a perfectionist, too. (Think of how we could get the world back on track.) I've mellowed over the years, but this ugly side of me appears whenever I'm not walking closely with my Lord.

I'm the answer to Patsy's prayers. I'm not what she prayed for, but I'm the answer she got.

My standard response when Patsy calls me on this is, "But I can explain!" And that is part of the problem. As a counselor friend put it, "Our tendency as men is to take on a lawyer role and logic our wives to death." The browbeater can always explain. That verbal skill is the key ingredient that makes him a browbeater in the first place.

I am verbal/aggressive and Patsy is nonverbal/passive. This not-uncommon combination is a nuclear holocaust waiting to happen. When an aggressive verbal husband says something to his wife, for him it's said, done, and over with. He's ready to move on. He thinks he has dealt with "a problem."

Our tendency as men is to take on a lawyer role and logic our wives to death.

One prickly predicament, however. When he says that "something" to a passive nonverbal wife, she tends to take it very personally. He thinks he's talking about "a problem" but she hears him talking about "a person"—her. He's ready to move on, but she can't let it go.

Patsy has taken many of the things I have said over the years to mean a conditional acceptance of her as "a person." I make her feel that she can't measure up to my expectations— that she can't meet my performance standards. That's not what I mean to happen ... but that's what she hears.

Whiners

Michael and I must see each other regularly because of an ongoing business relationship. Yet every time I think about being around him I cringe. Michael is a world-class whiner.

Whiners are verbal—they know how to talk. But they are not particularly aggressive. Rather than tackling a problem head on, the whiner would rather grouse and gripe and complain. He wants to avoid conflict, but he still wants to talk about it. This leads to you, his wife. Whiners want to rehearse all the slights, real and perceived, and all the grievances against them they don't want to address directly.

Just because whiners are not aggressive, don't think for a moment they are not angry. Grumblers are not happy campers because they are basically negative people.

The whiner has "poor me" disease. The world is out to get him. The people he whines to about his problems are usually the ones who can't do anything about them. Sometimes the whiner turns up the volume and not only complains about others, but whines about his wife to her face.

One man said, "My first tendency has always been to dump my problems on my wife. I have been learning to take things to the Lord. The Bible says, 'Cast all your care on him.'"

Someone has said, "Groan, but don't grumble." That makes good theology. As we wait for heaven we groan inwardly. Yet everywhere in Scripture, grumbling has always been a sign of disobedience and lack of faith.

Neglecters

In the early years of his marriage David, who owns a construction company, got involved with alcohol, drugs, and womanizing. He said, "I accommodated all of my natural inclinations." David had a life-changing encounter with God. Today his marriage is rock solid.

David reflected, "If I communicate with her daily and cherish my wife, life is great. But it's not natural for me to do it. She'll have to remind me. Then I'll make the adjustment. But I am a weak man who needs those reminders. And I don't chafe at them. I appreciate her telling me."

Neglecters are nonverbal. Sometimes their wives wonder what they can possibly do to get more than a grunt from these husbands. Neglecters can be passive/aggressive (e.g., foot dragging, not responding when spoken to, skipping chores or errands promised). But they usually are not shy about being openly aggressive. In other words, neglecters don't sit around and pout—they get what they want. They lay down the law and expect it to be kept.

Scott says, "Early in our marriage I was dogmatic about my word. But I couldn't communicate. I would experience frustration, get mad and then, because I really didn't know how to express myself, I would withdraw and separate from the family.

"Fortunately for me, my wife taught me how to communicate. Now, every night at dinner is an open forum for communication. Anyone can bring up anything, and I'm not allowed to jump on them. I have to listen and then respond constructively. It's made a huge difference in the 'feel' of our family life."

Scott's daughter, Leslie, found a man just like her dad. She fell in love and they became engaged. But last year she broke off the engagement. As Scott put it, "He was just like I used to be. He would put his head in the sand and just not deal with things. There is one difference between the two of us, though. While I was unable to communicate but willing, he wasn't even willing to try."

Bob said, "I have neglected my wife for so many years. As men we often have the tendency to put everything before our wives—building the business, building the church, building the kids, building the community, but we don't build our wives. This summer my kids spent several weeks with our extended family up north. It was a special time to build my wife. It's been a tremendous time of getting to know each other at a deeper level. I can't believe I neglected this so long."

Pouters

A woman was in counseling and the counselor asked her, "Do you wake up grumpy in the morning?"

She said, "No, I usually try to let him sleep in."

Pouters are nonverbal whiners. Pouters are just as negative and passive as whiners, but they don't like to talk about it.

Ben secretly resented his wife for what he considered a weak sex life. His way of dealing with it was to refuse helping with chores around the house. He told his wife, "I put in all the effort I can at work, so [he thought, *since you don't have time for sex*] you're just going to have to take care of the house." This is a type of passive-aggressive behavior. It has the appearance of passivity, but it is an aggression of its own.

A woman was in counseling and the counselor asked her, "Do you wake up grumpy in the morning?" She said, "No, I usually try to let him sleep in."

If whiners are "poor me's" then pouters are "victims." This husband often has his identity wrapped up in his work, so how he "is" depends on how his day went at work. Because he is nonverbal and passive, he often gets overlooked at the office or on the job. This makes him a sourpuss to live with because he won't deal constructively with his problems and frustrations.

Abusers

We have discussed the difference between a "normal" husband who can be difficult and a "difficult" husband. When does a "difficult" husband become an "abusive" husband?

If a man strikes his wife once, he is a suspected abuser. If he ever does it again, he is an abuser. This may sound too stiff, but a real man will never strike a woman. If your husband strikes you, or you have a friend whose husband strikes her, there can be no sugarcoating it. That man is an abuser, and he needs professional help. You or your friend may need professional help too.

If a man says things to his wife that no man should ever say to a woman he is a fool. However, if he does it regularly he is more than a fool, he is a verbal abuser. If you are afraid of your husband when he yells and loses his temper, and this is an everyday experience, he has more than an everyday problem. You should visit with your pastor or a professional counselor to learn how you can help your husband and yourself.

HEALING A DIFFICULT MARRIAGE

*U*ltimately, the healing of a marriage to a difficult husband involves a spiritual commitment. Without the guidance of the Bible, marriage is relegated to the standard of whim and personal opinion which, of course, changes like the direction of the winds.

The Bible exhorts husbands (and wives):

- "Husbands, in the same way be considerate as you live with your wives, and treat them with respect as the weaker partner" (1 Peter 3:7).
- "Do not let any unwholesome talk come out of your mouths, but only what is helpful for building others up according to their needs, that it may benefit those who listen" (Ephesians 4:29).
- "Love is patient, love is kind. It does not envy, it does not boast, it is not proud. It is not rude, it is not self-seeking, it is not easily angered, it keeps no record of wrongs. Love does not delight in evil but rejoices with the truth. It always protects, always trusts, always hopes, always perseveres. Love never fails" (1 Corinthians 13:4–7).

Our relationship changed when my wife saw me get serious about my relationship with the Lord.

As more and more husbands are exposed to these truths, they are making significant decisions to change their lives.

Ken said, "Our relationship changed when my wife saw me get serious about my relationship with the Lord."

Al said, "My wife can see a difference when I have been in the company of godly men."

And as these men choose to be "doers of the Word and not hearers only," they put their decisions into practice and begin to heal their marriages.

HOW YOU CAN HELP YOUR HUSBAND

Based on what men have been telling us, you probably are, or have been, living with a difficult husband. Yet, he is a husband who most likely has it in his heart to do the right thing.

He may be a browbeater, a whiner, a neglecter, or a pouter. What should be your reasonable expectations after reading this chapter?

You should prepare yourself for two possibilities: Either your husband will change or he will not.

What can you do to help your husband change? The spiritual answer is that only God's grace can change a man, and you can best seek that through prayer. The practical answer is that he must be confronted in love with his sinful behavior. Perhaps you need some counseling to know how to do this. You will need to insist that he treat you respectfully as an expression of his duty to love and nurture you.

If your husband is convicted of his sin and he changes, rejoice.

If he doesn't immediately respond, continue in faith to help him gain self-control. Some of us are a little slow. One male counselor tells women, "I really feel for you having to live with us men. We are dense. If we haven't heard about it today we think it must be fixed."

Many husbands will not change. They are selfish and are not yet ready to submit to biblical principles of love and marriage. You must prepare yourself for that possibility.

If your husband is not going to change then you must learn how to cope. Don't let him pull you down. Don't be a codependent. In other words, don't let his problem become your problem. A codependent response would be if your husband wrongly gets mad and blames you, and you accept the blame. Don't let your difficult husband ruin your day.

The Bible offers a clear, though demanding, direction to the wives of difficult men: "Wives, in the same way [as Christ] be submissive to your husbands so that, if any of them do not believe the word, they may be won over without words by the behavior of their wives, when they see the purity and reverence of your lives" (1 Peter 3:1–2).

A THOUGHT FOR HUSBANDS

𝒱irtually all men will admit that they are, or have been, a difficult husband to live with. I admit it. Have you been a difficult husband?

How can you tell for sure whether or not you are a difficult husband? Here are two test questions to ask yourself:

- The Chronic Test: Am I chronically difficult? Do I use anger and/or withdrawal as weapons on a daily or near daily basis?
- The Embarrassment Test: Would I be embarrassed for people to know how I treat my wife in private?

If you have answered "yes" to either question, you can be pretty sure your wife finds you difficult to live with. Let me encourage you to read this chapter and pray God would show you what to do. Perhaps you could meet with a friend or a counselor to talk it through.

As husbands we must take a leadership role to overcome our "difficultness." What's at stake when we are difficult is intimacy and connection with the only person in the whole world who is really in this thing with us together. Failure here is a price too high.

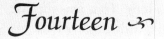

Fourteen

Perspective
Why Your Husband May Not Be As Bad As You Think

One Saturday morning a husband and wife were lingering over the morning paper and a second cup of coffee.

Seemingly from nowhere he blurted out, "I'm a failure as your husband."

"Why in the world would you say that?" she said. "You're not a failure. You're a wonderful husband."

"Well, that's not the way I feel inside," he responded.

"Honey," she said, "how could you possibly feel that way?"

"I don't know, but that's the way I feel."

The next sixty minutes were at once the most agonizing and profitable minutes of their marriage.

Over many years he had slowly come to believe that the repeated complaints of his wife were the defining realities of their marriage. He said, "For all these years we've been married you have repeatedly told me you don't feel connected to me because I don't do enough things with you. You've said you don't feel like I talk enough. I've really let you down, and I've failed miserably as your husband."

She was stunned. Her husband a failure? That was the last thought on her mind. Yet, as they talked through where his feelings were coming from, she had an "aha!" experience. It dawned on her that she had not expressed enough appreciation for the qualities in her husband she admired. In fact, in a moment of true humility, she admitted to herself that she had viewed her husband in an unfair way.

It occurred to her that ninety-five percent of the relationship was good. Not just good, but great. She drew a circle on a piece of paper and then drew in a slice of pie that took up about five percent of the total.

It occurred to her, "I have proportionately focused too much on the small slice of our relationship that is not working well, and not enough on that part that is working well. I've spent fifty percent of my time dwelling on five percent of our relationship."

She came to realize that, in perspective, her complaints were not as big of a problem as she had once thought.

She realized that she was too much of a perfectionist. She was asking for more than any man could do.

She also realized that she did not express verbal appreciation often enough for the things her husband did so well. In fact, when she was honest about it, she acknowledged to herself that she took these good qualities for granted and hardly thought of them at all.

Right then and there, she made a list of the qualities about her husband that she appreciated which came to mind. It was a long list. She was chagrined she had not told him more often of her feelings of appreciation. But she resolved to tell him right then. She said, "Honey, I really do appreciate and love you so much. I confess that I have not shown verbal appreciation to you often enough."

Then she continued to tell him the things she did appreciate, pausing after each item:

"I appreciate your willingness to listen to me.

"You give me feedback on how I'm doing with the kids.

"You do a tremendous job as the father of our children.

"You laugh at my jokes.

"You let me test out my crazy ideas on you.

"You do your work with excellence.

"You are a good provider to the children and me.

"I *know* that you love me.

"You are level-headed.

"I know you do want to be with me.

"You are extremely wise in the practical parts of everyday life.

"You're no failure. You're a terrific husband."

We tend to remember the good things we do, but forget the good things our mates do.

By the time she finished large tears streamed down through the creases on his face. He deeply appreciated her affirmations. They meant so much to him.

As she watched her husband weep, she realized how blind she had been. She had lost perspective of the big picture of her marriage to this man. Indeed, reading this list to her husband opened her own eyes to see things she had forgotten. When she saw how deeply these kind words touched her dear husband, she knew that this verbal appreciation had been long overdue.

TENDENCIES OF HUMAN NATURE

In the days that followed she reflected on some of the tendencies of human nature that are especially harmful to our marriages.

First, we tend to remember the good things we do, but forget the good things our mates do. At the same time, we tend

In marriage, it's important to objectively give your husband credit for growth and change where credit is due.

to forget the mistakes we make, but remember the mistakes of our mates.

Second, we tend to not recognize improvement in our mates. One of the biggest complaints teenagers have is that their moms and dads don't keep pace with how fast they grow up. Young executives bemoan superiors who remember them as they started, but don't give enough credit to how they have progressed. So in marriage, it's important to objectively give your husband credit for growth and change where credit is due.

Third, we tend to expect our mates to become something they will never be. There are many kinds of hammers, and they can be put to many kinds of uses. There are claw hammers, ballpeen hammers, reflex mallets, and jackhammers. They can drive nails, shape iron, fix dents, and break up concrete. There are many kinds of saws, and they can be put to many kinds of uses. There are wood saws, hacksaws, circular saws, band saws, and carbon saws. They can saw wood, steel, and glass. Both hammers and saws are useful tools, but a saw is always a saw and a hammer is always a hammer. You can't saw with a hammer, and you can't hammer with a saw.

A husband is a useful thing, but a husband is always a husband. There are some things your husband just can't do. Not now, not ever.

There are many kinds of men, and they can do many things. There are short men, tall men, bald men, quiet men, strong men, sensitive men. They can husband a wife, father a child, provide an income, and make a house a home. A husband is a useful thing, but a husband is always a husband. There are some things your husband just can't do. Not now, not ever.

All disappointment is the result of unmet expectations. If you feel disappointment with your husband, it's because your expectations of how he would love and care for you have gone unmet. If you have expected him to be able to be both hammer and saw, your expectations may need to be adjusted.

All disappointment is the result of unmet expectations.

HOW YOU CAN HELP YOUR HUSBAND

Suppose I could sit down with your husband for a few minutes and ask him, "How does your wife feel about you?"

How would he answer? Would he express feelings of unconditional love and acceptance? Or would he feel your love has strings attached? Would he feel respected by you? Or would his self-esteem be shaken somewhat by your second guessing?

Right now may I suggest you find a piece of paper and draw a circle, a pie, which represents your relationship with your husband. Draw a slice to the scale of what is not good in the relationship. How big is it? Consider the rest of the pie. Is the way you think of and speak to your husband proportioned to what's good about him and your relationship?

Why not make a list of all the things you appreciate about your husband. Here are some "trigger" words to stimulate your thoughts:

Integrity	Fidelity
Loving	Loyalty
Patience	Kindness
Good listener	Servant's heart
Humor	Man of prayer

Understanding	Flexibility
Dependability	Willing to share
Communication	Perseverance
Encourager	Hospitality
Faith	Spiritual leader
Accountable	Joyful
Survivor	Provider
Hard worker	Positive thinker
Nurturing	Compassionate
Stewardship	Humility
Helper	Intimate
Tolerant	Passionate
Even-tempered	Balanced
Sensitive	Accepting
Vision	Organized
Creative	Productive
Spiritual	Responsible
Commitment	Trustworthy

Make a date with him and tell him all the things on your list that you appreciate about him.

Finally, you may have contributed to a tension in your relationship because of overly high expectations. To set things on a new course you must decide to do so—you have to make a decision. If you feel comfortable with it, why not use the following suggested prayer, or one like it, as a way of committing to be more of an encourager to your husband.

Lord, I confess that I have dwelt too much on what's not working right in my marriage and not enough on what is working right. I've attached strings to this relationship that were never meant to be. God, you didn't make your love and acceptance of me conditional, yet I have made my love and acceptance of my husband conditional. I do love my husband, but I confess that I have not shown him enough respect for the many wonderful qualities he does possess. I have not given him enough credit for the effort he puts forth and the improvements he has made. I ask you to forgive and cleanse me. By faith I now make a decision to turn things around, to express verbal appreciation, to forget more mistakes, to forgive my husband, and to remember more good things about him. I will make whatever adjustments are needed for him to know that I love, respect, and appreciate him. Empower me by your Spirit to keep my commitment. Amen.

A THOUGHT FOR HUSBANDS

In this chapter I have shared with your wife the story of how one couple conquered some harmful tendencies of human nature. We need to realize that our wives really do love and appreciate us. However, they, like us, sometimes see the glass partially empty instead of mostly full. Be frank with your wife about any ways in which she can be more of an encourager and supporter to you.

Fifteen ~

Golden Years
Preparing for Winter

The following story sums up my marriage to Patsy, and probably your marriage too, if you have been married twenty or more years.

A couple was sitting in their den. He was reading the newspaper; she was reading a novel. After a good while she said, "Honey, go upstairs and put on a sweater."

"Yes, dear," he answered. He folded his paper, set it down on the ottoman, walked down the hall, up the stairs, opened a drawer, pulled out a cardigan sweater, and started back downstairs buttoning the sweater.

When he arrived at the doorway to the den he stopped and said, "Honey, can I ask you a question?"

"Yes, dear, of course" she answered. "What is it?"

"Are we going for a walk, or am I chilly?"

With age comes grace. And compatibility. And peace. And finishing each other's sentences.

In this final chapter I would like us to reflect on what husbands want their wives to know about what happens to them during the sweet, golden years of marriage—the run from "fifty to fifty." That is, from fifty years of age to fifty years of marriage. It is a precious portrait of hope and survival and a joyful vision to which younger couples can cling.

WHAT IT TOOK TO COME THIS FAR

Spring was a time for planting, roots taking hold, the blush of new growth, laying foundations, chasing dreams. With summer came building a home, forging the character of children on the anvil of life, developing a career, investing in a cause, a life task.

Now the children are grown and starting families of their own. You feel the cool breath of autumn against your face. You feel ... well, you feel pruned. Adjustments must be made. Yet, it is a wonderful grace that new cycles of growth always follow pruning.

Both husband and wife have made many sacrifices to come this far. Retirement is at hand, or will be soon enough. He is filled with thoughts of what could have been or what should have been.

He postponed building into his wife like he wanted during the years of building a career, raising children, and financing a lifestyle. But now he wants to turn his attention toward that woman who will slowly rock in the chair next to his.

He appreciates the contributions of his wife to raising the children, working for a second income, keeping the home together, and enabling him to pursue his calling.

They have survived a half dozen major tests.

She is the only one who knows his deepest thoughts.

She has been his long-term best friend.

Now he wants to make sure she will keep warm during winter. He wants to make up the years. He hopes to serve her the way she has served him. And his greatest desire is to bless her.

What happens to husbands when they feel the chilly gust of autumn?

REGRETS

$\mathcal{A}$ friend and his wife were attending a convention. After finishing a pleasant conversation with friends she stepped off the curb, was struck by a passing car, and died. My friend said, "I was going to build my organization. I was going to work hard. Then we would have time together. Now that will never be. I found out that life is paper thin."

By autumn all a man's regrets have come home to roost. The thoughts of what could have been and should have been weigh heavy on his heart. A husband desires to cease making regrets and start redeeming them.

Chief among regrets is the thought, "I wish I would have spent more time with my family." Billy Graham has said of all the things he could have done differently, he wishes he had spent more time at home.

Husbands often tell me, "I wish I would have been a strong spiritual leader in the home."

The falling leaves and barren trees of autumn remind a man of his unfinished business.

ENERGY

$\mathcal{F}$or over twenty years a late middle-aged man had prided himself on his capacity for work. He never took a break, and often took lunch at his desk or over a business appointment. He was athletic—the picture of physical fitness—but not as young as he once was. It was an emotional setback when one day, at the height of his career and physical fitness, he had to sit down for a moment of rest one day at work. For the first time in his life he felt the ticking of his body's clock.

It sneaks up on us men at the most awkward moments. We run for decades like a proud stallion. Yet one day while galloping along at full stride we see other stallions, younger stallions, high stepping past us. We're happy for them, but it still hurts. To see that you have lost a step is a startling realization.

In the days that follow we notice that our energy level is beginning to taper off. In due course we come to realize that our capacities are not what they once were. Over the span of a few restless years we are confronted by our own mortality. At first we chafe, but eventually a mellowing out takes place.

We realize we are not the young know-it-all bucks we used to be. (Sometimes, though, we think we are the wise old buck who *does* know it all.)

AMBITION

At the autumn accounting, your husband's ambitions begin to shift. He has had some wins and some losses. Now he wants to focus on achieving a success that matters.

All his strivings slow. Ambitions yield to calling. The desire to be successful yields to the desire to be faithful. He realizes that he is who he is. He ceases striving to achieve that which he was not meant to achieve. He no longer bristles when he thinks about the limits of his abilities. He begins to come to peace within and, thus, peace without.

A young man can contemplate these things from afar, but he will not truly know them until his own day of decline has begun.

DESIRES

Autumn. It's the season when a husband begins to cast about for a new vision—a different vision. A few dreams have come true, yet he accepts that not every oyster has a pearl.

Men are made for the task. They are driven to do the deed. Yet, as a man looks back over the littered landscape of his hopes and dreams, he observes that his life has been unbalanced. Sometime during autumn the desires of a husband begin to shift from *task* to *relationship*. In fact, in many ways the relationship becomes the task.

When husbands find themselves standing among the barren trunks of autumn, their regrets roost, their energy drops, their ambitions shift, and their desire for more "relationship" grows.

As he becomes more interested in building a deeper relationship with his mate, this comes as quite a shock to his wife who, in his absence, has built a life of her own. Maybe that's why the retirement quip, "For better or for worse, but not for lunch."

He glances to his side, and drinks long of his beloved wife. He sees her as he has never seen her before. He sees that she, too, is unsettled and vulnerable, and he longs to recover that which for so many years he set aside. Slowly, over time, a new dream begins to come clear, a better dream. It is the vision of two rocking chairs sitting side by side.

What changes do husbands want to make in their relationships with their wives to prepare for winter? Four key changes he wants to make include *more time, less pressure, enough money*, and *a best friend*.

MORE TIME

Bill was a traveling man most of his career. After the children left home he started taking his wife, Martha, on some of his overnighters. He would go to his appointments, and she would spend the day reading or shopping.

"It's been amazing," recalled Bill, "how many times Martha has mentioned how much those times meant to her. Little things do mean a lot."

When considering the changes he needs to make for winter, a husband wants to give his wife more—more time, more conversation, more companionship, more of what she needs.

The empty nest is a time of reconnecting when the kids are gone. It's not so much a new honeymoon, but a season to relearn each other. Later, when retirement comes, men think, *We need to take time now that there's time ... while there's still time.*

LESS PRESSURE

Early in our marriage," said Dave, "I pulled my wife into the rat race, and put her under the pressure of working to keep up a lifestyle. As a result, she didn't have as much time with the kids as she would have liked. I really want to make that up to her."

One important change husbands want to make in later life is to reduce the amount of pressure on their wives. When a husband ponders the many contributions of his wife, he wants to honor her by easing her way.

John, who is forty, encourages his wife to work the twelve- and thirteen-hour days demanded by her boss. It's okay with him because money constitutes a major focus of his life. Conversely, when Wayne, his next-door neighbor who is sixty, realized his wife was regularly required to work long hours, he saw the stress it caused and strongly urged her to quit. Many husbands who are wrongly motivated at thirty or forty years of age will see the light by fifty.

Frank has been retired for several years, but his wife, Lois, loves her job and has continued to work. She does not need to work for financial reasons, but enjoys the contribution she makes as the receptionist at a doctor's office. To bless her Frank takes care of all the household chores—a task he enjoys in return for all the years she served him so faithfully.

As husbands mature they begin to see value in lowering another kind of pressure too. It is the pressure to perform—to push both wife and children to live up to an overly high standard. When two of Scott's friends in their late forties died about the same time it caused him to reflect. He and his wife talked it over. He concluded, "I think we need to focus more on the good in our home, instead of disciplining all the time— go here, go there, do this, don't do that."

As men mature, grace replaces law as the rule of their hearts.

ENOUGH MONEY

A man piled his son and daughter into a small rented car and drove from Orlando to Raleigh, North Carolina, to pick up a beagle puppy.

On the return trip he was speeding along the interstate highway and came up too quickly on the rear of an eighteen wheeler. He swerved to miss the truck, but lost control of his steering. The car plowed through the median and smashed into a tree. He was not wearing a seat belt, was thrown from the car, and died instantly.

An elderly couple stopped their car to help, and discovered that both children and the puppy had survived the crash. They worked to free the boy, but could not get the girl out of the wreckage. Frantically, they tried to wave down passing motorists for help, but no one stopped.

Eventually an old man in a gray flannel shirt wearing a straw hat appeared. He began working to free the young girl, while the couple cared for the boy. Eventually he freed the girl, carried her to the tree where her brother was lying, and gently set her down. The couple fussed over her for a moment to get her settled, and then turned to thank the old man. He was gone.

This tragedy gripped our community. This man was a wonderful husband, a caring father, an outstanding layman, and a very successful businessman.

Yet the thing that impressed me the most was that though he died young, he provided for his family financially through insurance and savings. He had computed the real costs that his family would incur to maintain their lifestyle. They didn't have to sell their home. They didn't have to move into an apartment. His wife, a woman who worked in the home, didn't have to go into the job market.

In stark contrast, another man died suddenly and left his wife with tens of thousands of dollars in unsecured short-term debt. She had no potential to earn the kind of income needed to repay the debt. She loved her husband very much, but she is angry—seethingly angry—that he cared so little about what would happen to her. The pressure to repay her husband's debts preys on her mind.

As one man said, "A man who dies without putting his financial affairs in order hasn't merely left. He's absconded." It is a horrible, awful spectacle to see a woman radically alter her lifestyle because her deceased husband didn't provide for her financially. When a wife must sell her home, move into an apartment, and return to the job market at an age when she should be baby-sitting grandchildren, she was married to a selfish man.

As a husband hears the wind whistling through leafless trees, he takes steps to make sure she will keep warm during winter. Not only does he realize it's his responsibility, he knows that he is the only one who will do it. As one woman said, "If Lee died I don't know what I'd do. I know none of my brothers would come around to check on me or mow my grass. I'd be all alone." There are eight times more widows than widowers.

Not only do husbands want to make sure their wives are taken care of when they are gone, they also want to make sure they both will be taken care of if they live. One major unprepared-for illness can wipe out a lifetime of toil.

Recently a man observed, "With children living in distant cities and living fast-paced lives of their own, caring for elderly parents is less common today." For that reason he has been looking into insurance for long-term nursing home care.

A BEST FRIEND

John said, "Since I retired Mary and I have become best friends. Two months ago I had knee replacement surgery. As part of my therapy my doctor told me to walk twice a day. Mary has been walking in the mornings for years. She used to walk alone. Now we walk together and talk. It means so much to both of us."

Aaron said, "In the early years of our marriage we were husband and wife, now we're best friends and lovers. We have a 'ten minute rule.' If one of us is going to be more than ten minutes late we call each other. The other day I got to talking with someone and forgot to call. I was two hours late getting home and, boy, was Sally mad. That's because we love each other so much. I have always wanted to do the right thing by Sally, but in the first half of our marriage it was just superficial."

Julia had two married sisters who both died within the last two years. The first sister was married to an attentive husband and they had been completely devoted to one another. For a year and a half after her death, her widower, Ted, was lost and simply could not function.

The other sister had a difficult marriage marked by drinking, gambling, infidelity on both sides, and problems with their children. They were separated more than they were together. In spite of all their problems, after she was gone he said, "I'm lonely and she was a good woman." Incidentally, through it all he has come to faith.

Husbands come to the golden years with a considered understanding of how good their wives have been to them.

Honoring his wife and being her best friend looms foremost on a man's mind.

HOW YOU CAN HELP YOUR HUSBAND

A melody played in your heart during springtime and planting. You have weathered the sweltering heat of summer. Now it's time to harvest those years of sacrifice and toil. You've come a long way together. You've survived. It's the season to enjoy each other deeply.

Most husbands feel the burning sting of regret for what could have and should have been. Perhaps you could find it in your heart to forgive him for all the ways he's let you down.

He may be discouraged by the drop in his energy. Your unconditional acceptance of him as younger men pass him by will long be remembered.

As his ambitions change, signal your approval. When you see his desire for relationship increasing, don't be reluctant. Remember that this is the thing you wanted from the beginning.

Help your husband reconnect with you. You both will need to adjust your lives to spend more time together. Encourage him to reduce the pressure on you, as well as himself. Have a frank discussion about what will happen to you financially after he is gone. Also, talk over what happens if catastrophic illness should strike or long-term nursing care is needed.

Finally, be his best friend. Actually, you always have been. But he needs your reassurance from time to time.

A THOUGHT FOR HUSBANDS

*W*hat happens to men when they feel the cool breath of autumn? What changes does a man want to make in his relationship with his wife to prepare for winter?

When autumn arrives and regrets come home to roost, a man wants to stop making regrets and start redeeming them.

He experiences a lowering of his energy level. Yet, he comes to grips with his limitations, his mortality, and his diminishing capacities. He mellows out. His ambitions shift. He realizes that he is who he is, and does not chafe over the limits of his abilities. His desires change from *task* to wanting more *relationship* with his wife—a shock to this woman who has made a life of her own in his absence. What stage of life are you in? What has been happening to you?

Four changes that men want to make when preparing for winter include

- Spending more time with their wives
- Rearranging responsibilities so their wives are under less pressure
- Making sure there is enough money, whether he is still living or not
- Figuring out how to be her best friend

A man often postpones building into his wife during the years of building a career, raising children, and financing a lifestyle. During the autumn of life he wants to turn his attention to the faithful wife who will one day rock in the chair next to his.

He appreciates her contributions—raising the kids, working inside and outside the home, holding the family together, and enabling him to pursue his work. They have survived a half dozen major tests. She is the only one who knows his deepest thoughts. She has been his long-term best friend.

Now his greatest desire is to make sure she will keep warm during winter. He wants to make up the years of neglect. He wants to serve her as she has served him.

What thoughts and reflections come to mind about your own marriage? What are the changes you would like to make now, so that you can most enjoy rocking together when it's time? Is it ever too soon?

Afterword ᔄ

It is with no small degree of sadness that I bring this book to a close.

I deeply love my calling to help men—your husbands—think more deeply about their lives. Every day I see how these men struggle with the pressure of keeping, or putting, their lives together. The greatest struggle for men by far, though, is that their marriages are not working the way they are supposed to.

I wrote this book to help both you and your husband "break the code" on how to have the marriage you both dreamed about in those courting days when you first hinted around that you might want to spend your lives together.

The goal has been to tell you what a man is like from a man's perspective—to take you inside the locker room. I wanted you to know what he's going through, what he feels inside, and what's important to him. I pray you feel more emotionally connected to him and patient with him.

As I said in the introduction, marriage is a good thing. As your husbands, we know this. Yet we often get rattled by the demands and pace of this shrink-wrapped, rat-race culture in which we live and lose our bearings. Please forgive us. Most of us really do have it in our hearts to do the right thing.

The party will be over soon. The lights will dim. The crepe paper will droop down low. The party favors will be strewn about the floor. The children will be grown and gone. All your husband's golfing buddies will have moved to Florida to live in little condominium pods and drive around on streets made for golf carts. There will be only two rocking chairs left sitting side by side. Your husband increasingly realizes the importance of investing today in the person who will be sitting next to him then. Receive him when he does. Forgive and help him when he doesn't.

Marriage is a precious gift of God. It is my prayer for you that God will bless all your married days. May your husband become the man God wants him to be.

Acknowledgments ~

A work like this is the collective effort of thousands of people, mostly men, who have opened their hearts to share about their dreams and disappointments with vulnerability. I am forever indebted to the lessons they have learned and offered me the privilege of sharing with you.

A number of people reviewed the manuscript and profoundly improved the final book. Joe Creech offered the sensitive wisdom of an experienced marriage counselor. David Delk reflected on how to bring more richness to the concepts and principles presented. My editor, John Sloan, and the team of women readers he recruited, gave incredible input about how to make this book deliver what was promised.

My own wife, Patsy, reads everything I write and I can do nothing without her approval—I'm a lost puppy without her unwavering support. She challenged me on several points, and I yielded (eventually).

Without the help and encouragement of Robert Wolgemuth and Mike Hyatt I would surely have abandoned the idea for this book.

A special thank you to B. J. Belton, Betty Feiler, and Bill Miller for the sacrifices they made to give me the time I needed to write.

About the Author ✧

Business leader, author, and speaker Patrick Morley has been used throughout the world to help men and leaders think more deeply about their lives and to equip them to have a larger impact on the world. He has been the president or managing partner of fifty-nine companies and partnerships. He founded Morley Properties, which during the 1980s was one of Florida's one hundred largest privately-held companies.

Mr. Morley has also served as president or chairman of numerous civic and professional organizations. He serves on the board of directors of Campus Crusade for Christ and the editorial board of *New Man* magazine.

Mr. Morley graduated with honors from the University of Central Florida, which selected him to receive its Distinguished Alumnus Award in 1984. He is a graduate of the Harvard Graduate School of Business Owner/President Management Program and Reformed Theological Seminary.

Mr. Morley is the best-selling author of several books, including the award-winning *The Man in the Mirror* as well as *Walking with Christ in the Details of Life*, *The Rest of Your Life*, *Getting to Know the Man in the Mirror*, *Devotions for Couples*, *What Husbands Wish Their Wives Knew About Men*, and *Second Wind for the Second Half*. He teaches a weekly Bible study to 150 businessmen and leaders. He resides with his family in Orlando, Florida.

Notes ৵

ONE: Childhood—*"What I Know I Learned from My Dad"*

1. *The Orlando Sentinal,* June 13, 1996.

TWO: Significance—*What Is It That Your Husband Wants?*

1. Blaise Pascal, *Pensées,* translated by W. F. Trotter, 33. *Pascal, Great Books of the Western World* (Chicago: Encyclopedia Britannica, 1952), thought #425, 243–44.

2. Victor E. Frankl, *Man's Search for Meaning* (New York: Simon and Schuster, 1984), 105.

3. Michael Novak, *Business As a Calling* (New York: Free Press, 1996), 29.

THREE: Obstacles—*What's Troubling Your Husband?*

1. Frank Luska, "Oates relearns there's more to life than batting orders," *The Dallas Morning News,* June 5, 1995.

2. Patrick M. Morley, *Getting to Know the Man in the Mirror* (Grand Rapids: Zondervan, 1998), 1.

3. Several ideas in this chapter were first developed in a previous book, Patrick M. Morley, *The Seven Seasons of a Man's Life* (Grand Rapids: Zondervan, 1997).

4. Michael Novak, *Business As a Calling* (New York: Free Press, 1996), 6.

5. Francis A. Schaeffer, *How Should We Then Live?* (Westchester, Ill: Crossway, 1976), 205.

6. Aleksandr I. Solzhenitsyn, *A World Split Apart,* Commencement Address Delivered at Harvard University, June 8, 1978 (New York: Harper and Row, Publishers, 1978), 13.

7. This is an idea developed by Neil Postman in *Technopoly* (New York: Random House, 1992).

8. As quoted by Dr. William R. Bright.

9. Patrick M. Morley, *The Man in the Mirror* (Grand Rapids: Zondervan, 1997), 33.

FOUR: Pressure—*Understanding the Pressure Your Husband Feels*

1. Richard A. Swenson, *Margin* (Colorado Springs: NavPress Publishing Group, 1992), 15, 17, 91–92.

2. "As credit burden grows, many Americans may have reached their limit," *The Orlando Sentinel,* December 1, 1995.

3. Patrick M. Morley, *A Look in the Mirror, An Equipping Newsletter for Men* (Orlando: Man in the Mirror, 1995), Number 16.

4. Ralph Mattson and Arthur Miller, *Finding a Job You Can Love* (Nashville: Thomas Nelson, 1982), 123.

5. Bobb Biehl, *Stop Setting Goals* (Nashville: Moorings, 1995), 27–28.

SIX: Temptation—*The Six Persistent Temptations Men Struggle With*

1. Bob Buford, *Half Time* (Grand Rapids: Zondervan, 1994), 49–51.

2. R. C. Sproul, Gen Ed., *New Geneva Study Bible*, (Nashville: Thomas Nelson, 1995), 1767.

3. Patrick M. Morley, *A Look in the Mirror, An Equipping Newsletter for Men* (Orlando: Man in the Mirror, 1995), Number 16.

4. M. Scott Peck, *The Road Less Traveled* (New York: Simon and Schuster, 1978), 15.

5. S. I. McMillan, *None of These Diseases* (Old Tappan, NJ: Spire Books, 1986), 14.

SEVEN: Companionship—*What a Husband Needs from His Wife*

1. Ken R. Canfield, National Center for Fathering, "Promise Keepers' Sample, 1995 National Survey of Men, Report on 1995 Conference Attendees."
2. U. S. Bureau of the Census, *Statistical Abstract of the United States: 1995* (115th edition), Washington, D.C., 1995, Number 636.
3. Oswald Chambers, *My Utmost for His Highest* (Westwood: Barbour, 1963), 112.

EIGHT: Physical Intimacy—*What Else a Man Needs from His Wife*

1. The Orlando Sentinel, May 13, 1995.
2. Gary Smalley and John Trent, *The Gift of the Blessing* (Nashville: Nelson, 1993), 40.

NINE: Communication—*What Men Want to Express But Find Difficult*

1. Paul Tournier, *To Understand Each Other* (Atlanta: John Knox, 1962), 13–14.
2. I found the ideas discussed in this section and the next in Tournier, *To Understand.*

TEN: Resolving Conflict—*Help Around the House and Other Sore Spots*

1. David Seamands, *Healing for Damaged Emotions* (Wheaton: Victor, 1981), 107.
2. Tim LaHaye, *Understanding the Male Temperament* (Old Tappan, N.J.: Revell, 1977), 69.
3. Patrick M. Morley, *Devotions for Couples* (Grand Rapids: Zondervan, 1997), 68–69.

TWELVE: Fathering—*Your Husband's Changing View of Being a Dad*

1. Michael Novak, *Business as a Calling* (New York: The Free Press, 1996), 43.

2. Ross Campbell, *How To Really Love Your Child* (Wheaton: Victor, 1977), 45.

3. Ken R. Canfield, National Center for Fathering, "Promise Keepers' Sample 1995 National Survey of Men, Report on 1995 Conference Attendees."

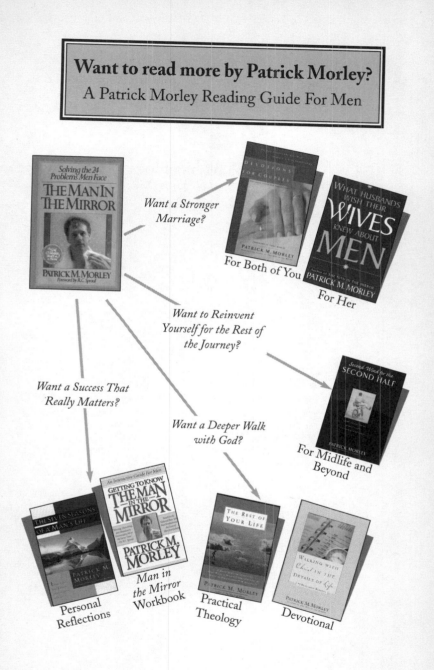

Want to read more by Patrick Morley?
A Patrick Morley Reading Guide For Men

Want a Stronger Marriage?

Solving the 24 Problems Men Face
THE MAN IN THE MIRROR
PATRICK M. MORLEY
Foreword by R.C. Sproul

DEVOTIONS FOR COUPLES
PATRICK M. MORLEY

For Both of You

WHAT HUSBANDS WISH THEIR **WIVES** KNEW ABOUT **MEN**
PATRICK M. MORLEY

For Her

Want to Reinvent Yourself for the Rest of the Journey?

Second Wind for the **SECOND HALF**
PATRICK MORLEY

For Midlife and Beyond

Want a Success That Really Matters?

Want a Deeper Walk with God?

THE SEVEN SEASONS OF A MAN'S LIFE
PATRICK M MORLEY

Personal Reflections

An Interactive Guide For Men
GETTING TO KNOW **THE MAN IN THE MIRROR**
PATRICK M. MORLEY

Man in the Mirror Workbook

THE REST OF YOUR LIFE
PATRICK M. MORLEY

Practical Theology

WALKING WITH Christ IN THE DETAILS OF Life
PATRICK M MORLEY

Devotional

We want to hear from you. Please send your comments about this book to us in care of the address below. Thank you.

ZondervanPublishingHouse
Grand Rapids, Michigan 49530
http://www.zondervan.com